DUPLICATES OF
TYPE SPECIMEN BOOKS, ETC.,
UNITED STATES AND FOREIGN

FOR SALE BY THE
TYPOGRAPHIC LIBRARY AND MUSEUM
OF THE
AMERICAN TYPE FOUNDERS CO.
300 Cumminpaw Avenue
JERSEY CITY, NEW JERSEY

OCTOBER, 1934

WITH
HISTORICAL NOTES AND COMMENTS
By HENRY LEWIS BULLEN

INTRODUCTION
By RICHARD B. YALE

WILDSIDE PRESS

LIMITED REPRINT EDITION – FIRST PRINTING

Printed in the United States of America

Library of Congress Catalog Card Number 72-72250

Hand bound by Jac Crawford and Richard B. Yale at
Mr. Crawford's private Valley Press.

INTRODUCTION

The Typographic Library and Museum of the American Type Founders Company at Jersey City, New Jersey was probably the finest of its kind in America. In 1936 the firm sold their Jersey City plant facility to a Chicago company and also sold the library to Columbia University.

Henry Lewis Bullen, the founder and curator of the Library and Museum, devoted forty years to assembling this collection, which gained world wide recognition. Bullen volunteered his services to manage the library without salary. It became his hobby to which he devoted all his spare time on holidays, Sunday's and at nights, while continuing his services as manager of certain production and manufacturing departments.

Mr. Bullen's association with American Type Founders began in 1892 and until 1895 he was the manager of the New York house of American Type Founders. The firm itself had been formed in 1892 by a consolidation of approximately 25 American type foundries. Most of these foundries had been deprived of their main sources of revenue because of the introduction of typesetting and typecasting machines.

In the consolidation most of the foundries continued to operate in their various cities under their original names. Several of the older foundries had assembled libraries for the use of their designers. McKellar, Smiths and Jordan had a library of several hundred books relating to typefounding. Other similar interesting libraries had been assembled by Bruce, Boston, Cincinnati, Dickinson and Chicago.

In 1895, Mr. Robert Wickham Nelson, third president of American Type Founders, promoted Mr. Bullen to general advertising manager and assistant general sales manager. By virtue of this new position Mr. Bullen acquired a certain amount of control over the various foundries and was permitted by Mr. Nelson to commandeer their several collections of books and periodicals relating to typefounding. These were brought to New York and, for lack of space at the general offices, were put in storage. The Jersey City plant was built in 1903 but it was not until 1908, and only then through the persistent efforts of Mr. Bullen, that the board of directors recognized the Library and Museum.

The collection, which was brought out of storage and combined with 300 books donated from Mr. Bullen's own personal library, was installed in new quarters at the Jersey City headquarters.

In a prospectus issued at the time the Board of Directors officially recognized the Typographic Library and Museum it was stated that such a library and museum "would attract to itself by bequest or purchase valuable collections which, under present conditions, are dispersed and fall into the hands of people inappreciative of their value." This prophecy was amply fulfilled.

The library acquired the extensive libraries assembled by Theodore Low DeVinne; that part of the library of David W. Bruce which related to typographic craftsmanship; a selection from the extensive library of the Typothetae of the City of New York; the century-old Boston Franklin Society library and several other similar collections.

Mr. Bullen resigned some of his duties with the company in 1923. He took time to visit similar collections in Europe and with the backing of Mr. Nelson proceeded to develop the American Type Founders Library to a completeness unequalled anywhere. Upon his return in 1925 the space assigned to the library was doubled.

With so many collections assembled into one there were bound to be many duplicates. None of these had ever been offered for sale.

The first of these duplicates was offered for sale in a 52-page catalogue issued, in 1934, 8½ x 11 inches, with chipboard back and a tan, embossed 65# cover, two wires at the top with kraft gummed tape binding. Despite all the type resources of American Type Founders Company, the catalogue was typed on stencils and mimeographed. Our reprint was reproduced and printed photo-offset.

The text has been reproduced complete. Do not get discouraged when you turn from page 20 and are looking at page 22. The typist in the original edition skipped 21.

The front matter of the catalogue is directed primarily to libraries and dealers in rare books. Mr. Bullen is calling their attention to the importance of type specimen books. He took particular pains in his historical notes throughout the catalogue to enhance the knowledge of the uninitiated.

It is these historical notes that make this catalogue so valuable today. Witness the surge in the number of hobbyists operating private presses today, the collectors of old presses, wood type fonts, wood engravings, specimen books and the many, many other facets of the printer's heritage.

Listed in the catalogue are forty-three American Type founders with a total of 136 specimen books described. In the Foreign section sixty-eight items are listed from thirty-five founderies. There are seventeen specimen books listed that were published by twelve printers. Under the title "Miscellaneous Typographica" fourteen more items are described.

This catalogue will be a great aid to collectors in identifying specimen books and gives a partial guide as to what to look for plus a ready reference to the history of the founderies themselves.

What Henry Lewis Bullen did for foundry types, Rob Roy Kelly has done in his magnificent volume on wood type. Published in 1969 and titled, "American Wood Type: 1828-1900," Kelly has assembled eleven years of research into a fascinating history of this facet of the American printing industry.

Andrew King, 86 years young, visited San Diego in February, 1972. Mr. King at one time had the only poster print house in Canada at Estevan, Saskatchewan. His wood fonts ranged up to 24 inches high. Circus and show posters were their specialty. He had wood engravers who cut illustrations on basswood up to three feet in height. I asked him if these cuts and the wood type were still available. The answer was no. Mr. King had sold the plant, which also published **The Estevan Mercury.** The new owners were only interested in the newspaper business. Canada is a cold country and wood type was excellent fuel for the furnaces. Only about 15 of the wood engravings were rescued by a former employee of Mr. King's.

Several years ago the Scioto Sign Company in Kenton, Ohio discontinued letterpress printing and converted to a silk screen operation. I was in Ohio shortly after this and learned they had given all the wood type and letterpress material to a job printer in a nearby small town. I contacted him and he still had the wood type. I stood in his basement on a hot August day and bought eighteen cartons of wood type, shipping weight 750 pounds; when I unpacked it in California I had some 320 fonts. Where I stood and bought the type was in front of the printer's Holland furnace. December would have been too late.

In the 1890's Henry Lewis Bullen had the foresight and sense of history to preserve, collect and perpetuate. In his time, linecasting machines created vast changes and in our time automation and computerization are making even greater changes. Let's hope the pace isn't so fast that tradition itself is killed.

Blake Clark wrote, "A nation with no regard for its past will have little future worth remembering."

RICHARD B. YALE, Curator
The San Diego Union Newspaper Museum

THE RECORD OF HENRY LEWIS BULLEN

Henry Lewis Bullen, founder and collector of the Typographic Library and Museum of the American Typefounders Company was listed as follows in Gustafson's "Who's Who in Printing in the United States and Canada, Part I:"

Henry Lewis Bullen was born at Ballarat, Victoria, Australia, September 18, 1857. [Died April 27, 1936] Training in typography, lithography and bookbinding in Australia, 1871-75; compositor in Davenport, St. Louis, Philadelphia, Trenton, New York City and Boston, 1875-80; Boston, salesman of printing and advertising and editor of house organ of machinery manufacturer and dealer in printers' supplies 1881-83; sales and advertising manager, 1883-88.

World tour developing export business in printing machinery and supplies, 1888-91; American Type Founders Company, 1892-1936; manager New York selling house, first advertising manager and assistant to general sales manager, originator and manager engineering department, founder and curator of Typographic Library and Museum, manager emeritus advertising and engineering departments, chairman committee on type designs.

Author of: "Theodore Low DeVinne," 1915; "Nicholaus Jensen, Printer of Venice," 1926; "The Nuremberg Chronicle" — a Monograph, 1930; "Printing and Civilization," 1923; "The Psychology of Printing Types," 1931; "The Greatness of Benjamin Franklin," "Pictorial Life of Benjamin Franklin," 1923; Editor "Collectanea Typographia," Inland Printer, 1918-25, 1928-30. Serial articles: "Discursions of a Retired Printer," Inland Printer, 1906-7; "Notes Toward the Study of Printing Types," The Graphic Arts, 1911-12; "The Literature of Typography," Inland Printer, 1912-16; "Printers' Avocations," Printing Art, 1918; "Biographies of Famous Printers," Inland Printer, 1920-22; "A Retrospect of Forty Fruitful Years," Inland Printer, 1923; "Advent of Type Composing Machines," Inland Printer, 1924.

Inventor of: Little Giant Brass Rule and Lead Cutter, Standard Job Composing Stick (both patented by Golding & Co., Boston). Designer: Cut Cost and Unit Systems of Composing-Room Equipments made for American Typefounders Co., by Hamilton Manufacturing Company. Promoter of vogue for Caslon, Cloister Old Style, and Garamound types inaugurating the Classic period of type design. One of founders of school for Printers' Apprentices of the City of New York, 1911.

DUPLICATES OF TYPE SPECIMEN BOOKS, ETC.,

UNITED STATES AND FOREIGN,

for sale by the

TYPOGRAPHIC LIBRARY AND MUSEUM of the

AMERICAN TYPE FOUNDERS COMPANY,

300 Communipaw Avenue,

Jersey City, New Jersey.

Telephone. Delaware 3-5000.

October, 1934.

TYPE SPECIMEN BOOKS FOR SALE

The following items are duplicates offered for sale by the Typographic Library and Museum, 300 Communipaw Avenue, Jersey City, New Jersey. Telephone Delaware 3-5000. Ask for Mr. Bullen.

Discounts to libraries and dealers in rare books will be quoted on request; to other buyers the prices are net, post or freight prepaid in the United States.

A Duty Performed

The founder of the Typographic Library, knowing the rarity of these duplicates, deems it his duty to put them in the way of being preserved. He wishes to interest the libraries and dealers, in the belief that when these books are catalogued by the dealers a demand will be created that will be met by the rescue of other copies from obscurity. He is confident that the study of type specimen books and the literature thereof will induce new and profitable avenues of approach to collectors. The librarian of the Typographic Library will willingly give dealers and librarians any assistance they desire in this matter. That there is an interest worth cultivating is proven by the fact that Daniel Berkeley Updike's learned, classic, and thoroughly well illustrated book, "Printing Types: their history, forms and use; a study of survivals, Cambridge Harvard University Press, 1922", 2 vols. pp. 611, is in its third edition. This and Birrell & Garnett's catalogue mentioned below, will be profitable reading for librarians and rare book dealers. The duplicates of specimen books here offered, will become, we hope, the bases of new, profitable, and useful avenues toward book collecting.

To Libraries and Dealers in Rare Books.--Typefounders' and printers' type specimen books and broadsides are now steadily increasing in interest as collectors' items. They are absolutely necessary to the increasing body of students of lettering for advertising purposes and for type designing. They satisfy many dilletante collectors because of their rarity, the comparative slowness of acquisition, and the limited number and extent of editions. The pleasures and expense of collections of these books may usually satisfy the collectors for a long term of years without burdening the shelves -- small, very interesting collections. For example: the choicest private collection of type specimen books in existence has been assembled by a diamond merchant in London, who otherwise has only a faint interest in typography. A small book case contains his accumulation of such books for several years. Incidentally, he has acquired a respect for the most vital implements of our present civilization -- printing types. His experience parallels that of another collector, a very wealthy man, not in any sense of the term a bookish man, who inherited a dozen Mathers, and discovering that they had great monetary value, and were eagerly searched for, became a collector of one of the most extensive collections of Matheriana, paying

To Libraries and Dealers in Rare Books

cheerfully thousands of dollars to acquire small rare items. He cares for no other books, yet he says that of all his other possessions he gets more satisfaction and pleasure from his small cabinet of Matheriana. He has a racing stable, but says he gets a greater thrill on finding another Mather than in winning the American Derby. Type specimen books and broadsides are infinitely more important than books by a Mather. Incidentally, the Matherianiac has become a good customer for printers and bookbinders. Progressive dealers in rare books are missing a profitable opportunity in neglecting to create an appreciation of type specimen books. The earliest type specimen was issued in 1486. The type specimen broadside of Ratdolt, issued in Augsburg in 1486, is accepted by authorities as a typographic masterpiece. The most beautiful type specimen book was issued by Derriey in Paris, in 1861. The specimen book of the American Type Founders Company issued in 1923, is a masterpiece. This company owns the finest and most complete collection of type specimen books and broadsides ever assembled. Printers who collect and study early type specimen books find in them a stimulus to pride in their most important artcraft that invariably improves their status in their occupation —witness De Vinne, Updike and Nash.

Several of the leading dealers abroad and two or three in the United States cater to the growing demand for these interesting books. A few issue special catalogues from time to time. The classic among such catalogues is that of Birrell & Garnett, Ltd., 30 Gerard Street, Soho, London, issued in 1928, an edition of 1750 copies. The demand caused the printing of an edition on special paper to sell for 10/6. It is a text book for type specimen book collectors and for booksellers who cater to them. Although it contains 252 rare items, our Typographic Library considers it to be a proof of the completeness of its type specimen collection that it possessed all those 252 items long before 1928. Since dealers abroad have given studious attention to type specimen books, the prices have risen, and many such books have been rescued from obscurity on unprofitable book shelves to meet an increased demand. A like result will be realized in the U.S. It is a fact that European type specimen books are now easier to collect than American issues. Our world-wide researches for type specimen books in the period, when such books were dead on booksellers' shelves, their cultural value and interest undiscovered. It is an acknowledged fact that our researches revived the interest in and created a profitable market for such books. In 1909 we issued a list of all the type specimen books we possessed on which it was announced in three languages that we were ready to buy any and all items, with successful results which surprised us, and continue in our favor. The American Type Founders Co. is a merger of all the type foundries in the U.S., some of them dating back to 1785, 1792, 1796, 1805, 1813 — 30 foundries in all. When the merger was effected, and a great central building erected in Jersey City to house the general offices and the central plant, all the type specimen books in the possession of those thirty foundries were sent to Jersey City. Thus was effected the nearest possible approach to a "corner" in type specimen books. Thus we came into possession of many duplicates, notwithstanding extensive sales by us to other libraries from time to time. The A.T.F. Co. has three collections of type specimen books: (1) In this library, which has made every effort toward a complete collection, American and foreign; (2) In the type foundry, for the use of the designing and production departments; (3) The duplicates now offered for sale, preferably to libraries and dealers in rare books.

U. S. TYPE SPECIMEN BOOKS

Early American type specimen books are now rarer than early European type specimen books. Such books published in the U.S. are printed for an industrial group to which (until lately) the instinct to preserve that distinguishes collectors is generally lacking. When new editions of the catalogues called specimen books were issued, the usual destination of the preceding edition has been the waste paper basket. On the other hand there is a steadily increasing appreciation of the value of out-of-print type specimen books to the growing group of students of lettering and the typographic art. Collectors rarely find any of the interesting items in the following list in bookseller's catalogues. Many of these items will find their place in the rare book class. The Typographic Library and Museum is the sole institution here or in Europe that has made a thorough effort to acquire type specimen books and broadsides, canvassing the whole world in this effort. Consequently this library has the most complete collection of type specimen books in existence, the earliest item (a broadside) dated in 1486.

The time is at hand when type specimen books will be in greater demand, and will merit the attention of rare book dealers. So far the Typographic Library has been able to satisfy the increasing demands of commercial artists, letterers, and typographic artists. Now this Library desires to effect a general clearance.

Condition of These Books

The condition of each item is stated. The bindings are seldom in first class condition. Many of them are scuffed, as is usual with text books and catalogues in constant use. The most important quality in second-hand type specimen books is that the contents shall be complete, in desirable good condition, and (if necessary) worthy of preservation and for that purpose worthy of repairing the covers or rebinding. Some of the items offered here are described as "sound", meaning that the contents and cover are without defects which would prevent their comfortable and safe use. However, to protect prospective buyers, who cannot examine a book before ordering, we agree that if any duplicate ordered without prior examination is found to have defects not reported in this list, or not reported in any letter describing the book written and received prior to date of order, it may be returned by means of transport nominated by us, after the alleged defects are reported to us; and upon receipt of said book, and we are at fault, the purchase price shall be quickly refunded. This offer applies only to type specimen books. As an example of the condition of certain duplicates, take the item Bruce, 1878 (837). The contents are complete, as described, the edges of the paper slightly discolored by handling; the covers are scuffed and loose at the back, though not detached. However, this is a notable, very rare and desirable book, well worthy of repairing or rebinding. When the binders charges are added to our price of $20, there is good value to the purchaser and great rarity. A little expense of bookbinding will easily transform this to a collector's item, satisfying the fastidious buyer.

Items of American and European origin are arranged alphabetically in four classifications.

Sizes. When an item is without pagination, the thickness of the book is given.

Historical Notes

Special attention is directed to the historical notes. Where lists of specimen books issued by various type foundries are given, they refer only to books on our shelves. When dealers in rare books sense the importance of type specimen books and catalogue them, other issues than those listed will gradually desert the shelves of old attics and old printing houses.

American Type Founders Co. Collective Specimen Book, New York edition, Oct. 1895 (774). Lge 4to. pp.752.................................$14.50

Cloth shabby, contents complete and in good condition.

First book issued by the American Type Founders Co. This Company was a merger in 1892 of the principal type founders of the United States. In its earlier years the consolidated type foundries used the type specimen books local to each section of the U.S., and did not issue a type specimen of a collective character until Oct. 1895 (the item above). The Collective Specimen Book was issued in various editions, with slightly differing arrangements, for various geographical areas. All editions are alike in the type specimens, differing only in such minor items as brass rules, etc. The name of the originating type foundry is printed with the specimens in a majority of instances. The Collective Specimen Book, whatever the edition, is important to the student of type faces, as it contains specimens of all the type faces which were most used in 1895, and all the type faces added after Nov. 1892, including the William Morris designs, Jensen Old Style and Satanick, which in a short time were to change and make obsolete nearly all the type faces made in the U.S. The Morris type faces were the precursors of the Classic Period of Typography. It may be noted that several of the type faces thus made obsolete have been revived in this New Era.

American Type Founders Company. Libro de Muestras de Tipos (786) New York and Philadelphia, Dec. 1896 8 vo. pp. 488 ....$ 5.00

First type specimen book especially printed in any country for Spanish-American trade; all types furnished with accents; explanatory matter in Spanish. Cloth, excellent condition, handsomely printed.

American Type Founders Co. (778) Specimens of Printing Types. New York, April, 1897, 8 vo. pp. 507 ....$ 5.00

Cloth, excellent condition; handsomely printed; complete.

American Type Founders Co. (780) Specimens of Printing Types
Philadelphia, Feb. 1898, 8 vo. pp. 522 .... $ 6.00

American Type Founders Co. (776) Compact Specimen Book. Specimens
of Printing Types. Philadelphia, March 1897, 8 vo. pp.522.... 6.00
Cloth excellent condition, handsomely printed, complete.

American Type Founders Co. (781) Handy Specimen Book. Chicago
1899, crown 8 vo. pp.918. Has illus. catalogue on pp.768
to 918 .... 4.75
Cloth, good condition; well printed; complete

American Type Founders Co. (782) Handy Specimen Book. Philadelphia
1899; demy 8 vo. pp.673, illus. catalogue on pp.515 to 673....4.00
Cloth, fair condition; complete.

American Type Founders Co. (785) Twentieth Century Desk Book
of Type Specimens...Catalogue of Printing Machinery and
Supplies. Printed in Philadelphia (for Minneapolis), Oct.
1900, demy 8 vo. pp.1184 ....5.25
Cloth, good condition.

American Type Founders Co. (783) Desk Book. Specimens of Type
Catalogue of Printing Machinery and Supplies; Printed in
Philadelphia (for St. Louis); 1899, demy 8 vo. pp.1024........5.75
Cloth, good condition; includes Useful Information for Printers
and Price List of Printing and Binding, a Guide for Charging,
compiled by Howard Ramaley; complete.

American Type Founders Co. (790) a desk Book of Printing Types
and Condensed Catalogue and Price List of Printing Machinery
and Materials. Printed and issued in Boston for use in New
England territory only; 1898, crown 8 vo. pp.946 ....5.00
Cloth, excellent condition; a model book; includes useful
Information for Printers and suggested Price List of Printing and
Binding; all illus. in outline.

American Type Founders Co. (792) Mostrario de Tipos. Todo cuanto necessita el Impresor. Printed in Philadelphia for distribution in Spanish America, 1907, demy 8 vo. pp.800 .... $ 4.75

Cloth, good condition, handsomely printed, complete

American Type Founders Co. (788) Specimen Book of American Line Type Faces. American Point Line, Point Body and Point Set. Jersey City, (1904) 4to.pp. 292 .... 2.50

First American point line book, with diagramatic explanation of the point line system. First specimen book printed in Jersey City plant. Cloth, good condition.

American Type Founders Co. (793) American (point) Line Type Book Price list of Printing Material and Machinery. Jersey City 1906, demy 8 vo. pp.1181 .... 6.00

First complete American point line book. Cloth, good condition
Beginning with 1904 all American Type Specimen Books, catalogues, and other printings were printed and issued from the specimen printing department of the Central Plant, for the use of all the Company's selling houses and agencies.

American Type Founders Co. (794) American Line Book. Jersey City, 1906; demy 8 vo. pp.920 .... 4.50

This, so far as types are concerned, is precisely the same as preceding item, the catalogue of printing machinery and materials being omitted. Cloth, good condition.

American Type Founders Co. (795) Supplement to the American (Point) Line Type Book (of 1906) Jersey City, 1909; demy 8 vo. pp.246... 1.25

Paper, fair condition; contains new type faces and ornaments, or additional sizes of such material, added since 1906.

American Type Founders Co. (796) American Specimen Book of Types,
with complete catalogue of Printing Machinery and Printing
Supplies. Jersey City, 1912; imperial 8 vo. pp.1301.......... $ 15.00
Half mor., gilt edges; a fine book, showing little signs
of wear; complete.

American Type Founders Co. (799) Supplement to American Specimen
Book of 1912. New Type Styles, Ornaments and Brass Rules.
Jersey City, 1917; imperial 8 vo. pp. 215..................... 1.25
Paper, good condition; complete; exhibits the novelties of
five years of effort.

American Type Founders Co. (798) Specimen and Price List of Brass
Types and ornaments and Brass Rule for Bookbinders' use.
Jersey City, 1907; 8 vo. pp. 90 .... 1.35
Half cloth; sound condition.

American Type Founders Co. (629-47) Desk Book of Type Specimens
Catalogue of Printing Machinery and Printers' Supplies.
Philadelphia, 1900; 8 vo. pp. 1168 .... 9.50
Full mor., gilt edges, perfect condition, complete.

Barnhart Bros.& Spindler (629-50) Specimen Book and Price List
of the Great Western Type Foundry, B.B.& S. proprietors,
105-111 Madison St. Chicago, July, 1873; 8 vo. Specimens
printed on one side of paper only, no folios 15.00
The first specimen book of this important firm established
in 1872, the second greatest type foundry in the U.S. which in
1911 was merged with the American Type Founders Co. Cloth,
complete in good condition.

Barnhart Bros. & Spindler (805) Great Western Type Foundry. Pony
        Specimen Book and Price List, from B. B. & S., 183 to 187
        Munroe Street, Chicago, circa 1898; sm. 8 vo. pp.563 ....$ 3.75
        Cloth, sound condition.

Barnhart Bros. & Spindler (807) Specimen Book of Type (and
        Catalogue and Price List of Printing Machinery and
        Materials) Chicago, 1900; 4 to pp.880 .... 4.75
        Cloth, fair condition, sound, complete.

Barnhart Bros. & Spindler (808) Great Western Type Foundry
        Barnhart's Big Blue Book containing Specimens of superior
        copper mixed Type, Borders, Ornaments, etc. Chicago, circa
        1895; 4 to. pp.323 .... 4.25
        Cloth, fine condition, complete.

Benton, Waldo & Co. (814) Portable Book of Specimens from B. W. &
        Co, Type Founders. Patentees and manufacturers of Benton's
        Self Spacing Type. Milwaukee, circa 1884; 8 vo. pp.192........ 6.00
        This type foundry was begun in Albany N. Y. in 1826 by R.
Starr & Co., as the Albany Type Foundry. It changed owners a
few times. In 1847 its owner was J. T. Reton, who in 1854 took
it to Chicago. Reton, on arriving in Chicago was persuaded that
Milwaukee had a greater future than Chicago; consequently he did not
establish his foundry in the latter city; took it to Milwaukee,
where he sold it, under the name of Northwestern Type Foundry, to
J. A. Noonan, a paper maker. In 1866 Reton was an employee of
Noonan, managing the type foundry. The next that is known of Reton
is in Kansas City, where, in 1872, he began a type foundry. In
1873 Noonan failed, and his type and electrotype foundry were
purchased by Benton & Cramer, the latter the son of the publisher

of a Milwaukee daily paper. In 1874 Cramer withdrew; his half interest was purchased by F. M. Gove, the firm name changing to Benton, Gove & Co. In 1882 Gove died, and Benton became sole owner, selling a one third interest to R. V. Waldo in the same year. Gove and Waldo were utterly inexperienced, having no knowledge of type making or of printing. Benton in 1882 had only nine years experience of type making, but had an earlier experience in printing. When Benton became part owner in 1873 of the Great Western Type Foundry, it had the reputation of having the worst equipment in the business. With this seemingly meagre back-ground Linn Boyd Benton, as early as 1885, was conceded to be the greatest inventor in the history of type making. His inventions revolutionized the art. He became known in later years as "the Edison of type making". Benton, Waldo & Co. sold their foundry to the American Type Founders Co. in 1892, the new owners moving it to New York City in 1893; Benton becoming a director and manager of manufacturing of the American Type Founders Co. Of Benton inventions it is admitted that he made possible the success of the Monotype and Linotype inventions.

Specimens of type made by the firms named in the above brief history are exceedingly rare. The fact is that as type makers they had no celebrity until 1884, when Benton's "self spacing" types were patented. The book here offered is in cloth, complete, good condition, except that one signature is loose. It contains the picture of the B. W. & Co. foundry as it existed at the time of its sale. Here is the earliest description in book form, with specimens, of "self-spacing" types, all the characters cast on eight widths, including the italics, which are actually sloping romans.

Benton & Waldo Type Foundry (816) Portable Book of Specimens from
the B. & W. Foundry, operated by American Type Founders Co.
Milwaukee,,1893; 8 vo. pp.271 .... $ 4.50
Board cover, fair condition, complete. First book issued
under the ownership of the American Type Founders Company.

Binny & Ronaldson (82-1-3) Specimen of Printing Types, from the
Foundry of B & R., Philadelphia, Fry & Kammerer, Printers,
1812; 8½ x 5 in., 39 folios, printed on one side only,
no folios 135.00
Half morocco; original pasted paper cover bound in. One of
the only known three complete copies. This book was once the
property of F. Bradford, Jr., the first printer in Kentucky, at
Lexington; his autograph appears three times in this book.

First typefounders' specimen book issued in America. Binny &
Ronaldson began in 1796; in 1797 they acquired the typefounding
apparatus brought from Holland in 1791 by Adam Gerard Mappa, who was
the first to make type in New York, in 1806 they purchased from the
executors of B. F. Bache the typefounding apparatus brought to
Philadelphia from France in 1785 by Benjamin Franklin. However, they
did not issue a specimen book until 1812, their advertising of types
until that date being done with small broadsides. After 1806 their's
was the only typefounding concern in the U.S. They began with typefounding apparatus brought from Scotland by Binny, this was valued
at $880.00, to which James Ronaldson, a baker by trade, a shipmate
of Binny's added $880 in cash for a half interest. Archibald Binny
was a typefounder expert in all branches of that art. In 1815 James
Ronaldson paid Binny $62,000 for the latter's half interest, with
which, and money he had saved in 19 years, he bought an estate of
5000 acres, a mansion and 75 slaves. On this estate he lived until
his death in 1838. The estate, situated at the junction of St. Mary's
river and the Potomac river, in Maryland, had increased in value,
through good management. Binny was buried in the city of St. Mary's.
James Ronaldson continued the business profitably, investing his
profits in canals, anthracite coal mines, and city real estate.
In 1824 he became one of the founders of the Franklin Institute, now
world famous, of which he was the first president holding that office
until his death in 1841. His successors in typefounding were:
Richard Ronaldson, 1823-1833; Johnson & Smith, 1833-1843; Lawrence
Johnson, 1843-1845; Johnson & Co. 1845-1867; MacKellar, Smiths & Jordan,
1867-1892; American Type Founders Co., 1892, still continuing.

(Binny & Ronaldson) 1816 (82-1-10) Specimen of Printing Type, from the
Letter Foundry of James Ronaldson, successor to Binny &
Ronaldson, Cedar between Ninth and Tenth Streets, Philadelphia
1816 ....$130.00
Calfskin; good condition; complete; very rare.

(Binny & Ronaldson), 1822, (82-1-12). Specimen of Printing Type,
from the Letter Foundry of James Ronaldson, Successor to
Binny & Ronaldson, Cedar between Ninth and Tenth Streets,
Philadelphia; 1822 ....125.00
Half morocco; good condition; complete; very rare.

Binny, John (818) Specimen of Printing Types. S.E. Corner of Dock and
　　Second Streets, Philadelphia, 1841; 4to 50 folios printed on one
　　side only $35.00
　　　　Very rare, complete; covers loose, but original front paper cover
bound in; good condition. John Binny was the son of Archibald Binny
of Binny & Ronaldson (see historical note above.) John began as a
master typefounder in 1839, the year following the date of the death
of his father. Prior to that event he was employed as a punch cutter
by James Ronaldson. John issued two specimen books, one in 1839, a
slim affair, and the other in 1841, after which date he disappeared
from typographic history. This is one of the three known copies; an
interesting item.

Boston Type Foundry (629-53) Specimen of Modern Printing Types cast
　　at the Letter Foundry of the Boston Type and Stereotype Company,
　　No. 39 Congress Street. John G. Rogers, agent. Boston, 1837;
　　8 vo. $\frac{3}{4}$ in. thick 25.00
Original boards, good condition, complete.

　　The Boston Type Foundry, now merged with the Dickinson Type
Foundry, as the Boston selling house of the A.T.F. Co. was the first
type foundry in New England. It was begun as a branch of the type
foundry of Elihu White of New York in 1817 in Charlestown. In 1818
it was owned by Ewer & Bedlington, who moved it to Boston, where it had
an interesting history. It was in 1826, the first type foundry to
attempt the manufacture of types by machinery. It continued its efforts
in that direction for five years, after which it reverted to hand mould
casting. In 1844 it was the first type foundry to use the perfected
Bruce type casting machine, buying exclusive lease for its use in New
England in that year, after a period of successful demonstration. This
lease is now in the possession of the Typographic Library. Connected
with this type foundry were several names famous in the art: Lyman,
Starr, Conner, Pelouze, Phelps, Dalton, all of whom became owners of
type foundries. David Bruce, Jr., was employed as a letter punch cutter,
his first work being the admirable Hancock Script, which was superior
to any script in the old world, setting a standard of quality for scripts
that has been maintained in this country ever since. He was the inventor
of the first practicable type casting machine. In the early seventies
of last century the foundry opened a Branch factory in St. Louis under
the management of James A. St. John and Carl Schraubstadter, both of
them were stockholders in the Boston Foundry. They became owners of the
foundry in St. Louis continuing under the name of Central Type Foundry.
They prospered and in 1899 became owners of the parent type foundry,
which, in 1892, they sold to the American Type Founders Company, thus
closing an eventful and interesting history. This type foundry issued
type specimen books in 1820, 1825, 1826, 1828,1832,1837,1845,1853,1856,
1857,1860,1864,1867,1869, 1871,1874,1878,1880,1883,1884,1888,1889,1890(2).
All necessary to the study of printing types made in America.

Boston Type Foundry (629-52) Specimen of Modern Printing Types, cast at
　　the Letter Foundry of the Boston Type and Stereotype Foundry, Minots
　　Building, Spring Lane, corner of Devonshire Street, James M. Shute
　　agent. Boston, 1845; royal 8 vo. 2 ins. 20.00
Original half leather, sound condition, complete.

Boston Type Foundry (824) The oldest type foundry in New England. Established in 1817. Specimen Book from the Boston Type Foundry. J.A. St. John, agent; C. Schraubstadter, president; D. W. Rogers treasurer. Containing also a complete Price List of Printing Material. Boston, 104 Milk Street, corner Kilby Street, 1889; 4to., 1 in. thick $8.00
Original cloth, sound condition, complete, contains a selection of types made by the Central Type Foundry, St. Louis.

Boston Type Foundry (825½). Supplementary Specimens, B.T.F. John K. Rogers & Co., proprietors, Boston, 1857 .... 1.00
Boards, 4to. pp.32, printed on one side only; covers broken and loose; contents complete and in good condition.

Bresnan Type Foundry (826) Specimen Book of Types, Brass Rule and Printer's Material. P.H. Bresnan, Type Foundry and Printer's Warehouse, 201-205 William Street, New York. Second Title (on page 71); Bresnan Type Foundry. Specimens. New York 1896; 4to.pp.180...... 3.00
Cloth, good condition, complete.

The history of the Bresnan Type Foundry is curious. In 1856 S.R. Walker (who was a manufacturer of brass rules, dashes, and leads and slugs) and H. L. Pelouze (a type founder of recognized ability), formed a partnership and advertised a type foundry at 54 Ann Street, N. Y., issuing a specimen book in 1857. They established a type foundry at Richmond, Va., in 1859. The partnership was dissolved in 1860. When the Civil War began in 1861, Pelouze, a Federalist, attempted to remove his business to a Northern State. It was the only type foundry in the Confederate States. The Confederate Government sensing the importance of printing types to their cause, forbade his departure and he was forced to remain and make types until the close of the war. Walker died in 1866. He was succeeded by his son. In the early seventies of last century the Tweed Ring became owners of this type foundry, for reasons not divulged, and the manufacture of brass rules and sale of printing materials was continued by the firm of Walker, Bresnan & Tuthill (see next item). When the Tweed Ring was destroyed its type foundry became the property of its former owners, under the name of Walker & Bresnan. This firm was dissolved, and was succeeded by the P. H. Bresnan Type Founding Company. The foundry was dispersed when Bresnan died in 1895.

Bresnan (965) Specimen Book of Brass Rule, Circles, Dashes, etc., manufactured by Walker, Tuthill & Bresnan, New York, 1882; 4to, pp.44; specimens printed on one side only 2.25

Bruce, (629.55). A Specimen of Printing Types, cast by Geo. Bruce & Co. at 13 Chambers Street, Near Chatham Street, New York, 1837 .... 16.00
Original stamped cloth; covers loose; royal 8 vo; 1½ in. complete.

Decidedly the best American type specimen book of the period. Contains the earliest specimen of music types cast in America. These were cast on a simplified plan, original with this foundry, the notes in combination effected by thirty characters, all on one body, of the size of the space between the staffs. The staffs were of brass rules. The clefs are in three to five pieces. The effect, as printed in the specimens, are perfect; whether they printed as well after use is a

-12-

question. The use of the combinations require a good knowledge of music notation by the type setters. The double page broadside explanation will interest collectors of the literature of music. There is a price list. There is a striking collection of borders, many of them original; also many quaint stereotyped cuts. Well worth rebinding.

David and George Bruce, brothers, came to New York as journeymen printers, began business there in 1806. In 1813 they added stereotyping, being the second firm in America to employ that art. David, the elder, was inventive. He invented the plate shaving machine, the mahogany block for holding unmounted plates, and the box with sliding cover in which to transport unmounted plates safely. In 1813 the Bruce brothers bought the small type foundry of Edwin Starr and sold their printing business. In the same year they issued a small type specimen book adding to it yearly, until in 1818 these specimens filled a book half an inch thick. From this date they soon acquired leadership and wealth. In 1822 David, the elder partner, retired to an estate on the banks of the Delaware River, not far from Trenton. The business was continued with great success by George, who died in 1866, one of New York's wealthier citizens. He was succeeded by his only son, David Wolfe Bruce, who died in 1895, bequeathing the type foundry to three of his principal assistants Two of these retired in 1896; the third sold the type foundry in 1902 to the American Type Founders Co. The Bruce Type Foundry issued specimens in 1815, 1816,1818,1820,1821,1824 (George Solis), 1831, 1837 (the Co. was Peter C. Cortelyou, see below), 1841,1842,1848,1855 (George Solis), 1867, 1869 (2) a series of supplements issued yearly until 1878, 1881, 1882, a series of yearly supplements until 1889, 1900, 1901, 1903 (issued by the American Type Founders Co.) These all show yearly progress, and are indispensable to the study of typography, in America.

Bruce, 1853 (629.56) Bruce's New York Type Foundry. Established 1813.
    Specimen of Printing Types, etc., cast and made by George Bruce
    New York, Sept., 1853; No. 13 Chambers Street, City of New York......$10.00
    Cloth cover, loose, and back off; med 8 vo.; contents complete
and in fair condition. Interesting; well worth rebinding; four pages
of borders for printing in several colors.

Bruce, 1865 (629.57) An Abridged Specimen of Fonts of Type and Brass
    Printing Materials made at Bruce's New York Type Foundry. New
    York; George Bruce, Type Founder, No. 13 Chambers Street,
    November, 1865 .... 4.50
    Bruce's first quarto specimen book, pp.76, printed on one side
only; in good condition; boards, cloth back; complete.

Bruce, 1869 (832) An Abridged Specimen of Printing Types made at
    Bruce's New York Type Foundry. New York; George Bruce's Son & Co.,
    No. 13 Chambers Street, 1869, pp. 166, printed on one side only.
    Second Title: An illustrated and descriptive Priced List of
    Printing Presses, etc., made by Degener & Weiler, George P.
    Gordon, and R. Hoe & Co. all of New York. October 1868,pp.XIV.......... 7.50
    Edited and printed by Dr. Theodore Low De Vinne. The texts used
for specimen lines are authentic historical data relating to printing.
For example: P.58 consists of fourteen paragraphs containing a history
of stereotyping.
    Half leather and cloth; good condition; complete. This is a
monument to De Vinne's studiousness as a young man. It is a classic
among type specimen books.
    The "Co." in the title was James Lindsay, a distinguished Scotch
type founder who gave added distinction to the Bruce establishment.
(See Lindsay below)

Bruce, 1878 (837). First title: Specimen of printing types, made at
Bruce's New York Type Foundry, established in 1813. Vol. 1, New
York: Geo. Bruce's Son & Co., No. 13 Chambers Street, 1878. (This
title relates to all specimens of display types, pp.204). Second
title: The Invention of Printing. A collection of facts and
opinions descriptive of early prints and playing cards, the block
books of the fifteenth century, the legend of Laurens Janszoon
Coster, of Haarlem, and the work of John Gutenberg and his
associates. Illustrated with facsimiles of early types and wood
cuts, by Theo. L. De Vinne (A quotation from Fox's Acts and
Monuments.) New York: George Bruce's Son & Co. Type founders,
No. 13 Chambers Street, 1878 .... $ 22.50
Quarto, pp.372, all pages printed on one side only, complete;
half leather, one cover loose but not detached; contents in good condition. Vol.2 was not issued; as stated in the preface it was intended
to show in it the Bruce borders and other decorative material.

Contains the first issue of De Vinne's best-of-all histories of
the invention of printing in English, which in the same year was issued
in book form. The history is printed in full in this book, and is used to
exhibit the Bruce book types, each page showing one size, from Great
Primer No. 1 to Diamond No.16. George Bruce the younger was a generous
patron of De Vinne in his earlier career. The proceeds of the purchase
by Bruce of permission to use the complete manuscript of this famous
authentic history in his specimen book, enabled De Vinne to finance the
separate issue of the history in book format a few months later, in 1878.
De Vinne was also engaged to edit and print this notable type specimen
book, now rare. The edition in regular book format issued a few months
later is also extremely rare, for the reason that it was issued in paper
covers in parts to recipients without the booklovers conscience, who failed
to preserve them.

Duplicates

Bruce, 1882 (839). First title: Specimens of Printing Types made by
Bruce's New York Type Foundry. Established 1813. New York:
George Bruce's Son & Co., No. 13 Chambers Stre t, 1882. With
Supplements: First (April 1883), Second (July 1884), Third (July,1885),
Fourth (July, 1886), Fifth (May 1887) Sixth, (Jan.15,1889). Second
title: The invention of Printing: A collection of facts and opinions
descriptive of early prints and playing cards, the block books of
Coster of Haarlem, and the works of John Gutenberg and his
associates. Illustrated with facsimiles of early types and wood-
cuts. By Theo. L. De Vinne. (A quotation from Fox's Acts and
Monuments). New York; George Bruce's Son & Co. type founders,
No. 13 Chambers Street, 1878 ....50.00
The most notable type specimen book ever issued anywhere, very
rare. Edited and printed by Theodore L. De Vinne. Contains all that
was intended to be printed in vol. 2 of Bruce 1878, referred to in
description of item immediately above. Note above, referring to De Vinne's
classic history, refers also to this item. Contains specimens of all
the type faces made by the Bruces' since 1818. Also a description of the
system of type bodies originated by George Bruce in 1822. Also a complete
showing of Bruce's Celebrated Penman Scripts, the finest script series
ever made, a triumph of type making, but too elaborate and high-priced
to gain a good market;frontispiece copperplate portrait of George Bruce.

Large 4to. pp. 548; all pages printed on one side only. Cloth, leather back, scuffed, front cover loose, needs rebinding, and well worth it; contents complete and in good condition; weight $9\frac{1}{2}$ lbs.

Bruce, circa 1900 (842). Bruce Type Foundry. Handy Book of Types, Borders, Brass Rule, Cuts, Printing Machinery and General Supplies. Bruce Type Foundry, 13 Chambers Street, New York, U.S.A. no date .... $ 4.50
Cloth lge. 8 vo. pp.592; excellent condition.
This is the last book of the Bruce Type Foundry. It was issued by the A. T.F. Co. who bought it from V. B. Munson to whom it was bequeathed by David Bruce, Jr., in 1890. It contains specimens of the types of the Bruce manufacture deemed to be most salable in 1900. The pages with the imprint "V. B. Munson, Successor", are of Bruce manufacture; those minus the name of Munson are of the A.T.F. Co. manufacture. Well printed and interesting.

Baltimore Type Foundry, 1888 (846). Convenient Specimen Book of Types, Rules, Borders and Electrotype Cuts from the Baltimore Type Foundry, Chas. J. Cary & Co., Baltimore, Md., 1888 .... 3.00
Cloth, lge. 8vo. pp.368, complete, covers loose but not detached.
This foundry was begun in 1804 by Christopher Sower, followed by R.B. Spaulding (1818), F.Lucas, Jr.(1832), Lucas Bros.(1854), Henry Lucas (1860), F.H. Lucas(1872), Henry L. Pelouze & Son (1879), C. J. Cary & Co. (1883). Type specimsn were issued in 1832, 1851, 1854, 1879,1883, 1886, 1888.

Buffalo Type Foundry, 1889 (844), Established in 1835. Re-established in 1889. William E. Lyman, Carleton H. Lyman, Specimens of Printing Types made by the Buffalo Type Foundry. W. E. Lyman & Son, proprietors, Buffalo, N. Y. 1889 .... 2.25
Cloth, quarto, good condition, pp.178 with a number of leaves of specimens inserted after binding.
This foundry was established in 1834 by Nathan Lyman, who died in 1873. The business was carried on successively by his son and grandson. In 1888, the year the point system of type bodies was accepted by all American type foundries, the Buffalo Type Foundry equipment was abandoned and the foundry re-equipped. In 1892 it was sold to the A.T.F. Co. This foundry issued specimen books in 1841, 1853, 1879, 1889.

Central Type Foundry, 1886 (629.62) Price List of Types and Printing Materials. Central Type Foundry, Manufacturers of the Celebrated Copper Alloy Type. St. Louis; April, 1886 ....4.50
Boards, lge.4to., covers loose but not detached; pp.192, contents complete, in good condition.
This foundry began as a manufacturing branch of the Boston Type Foundry in 1872. Bought by St. John and Schraubstadter, stockholders in the B.T.F. in 1874. Very soon became noted for the originality of its type faces and quality of manufacture. In 1888 disputed leadership in type design with MacKellar, Smiths & Jordan of Philadelphia. In 1888 bought controlling interest in the Boston Type Foundry. In 1892 sold both foundries to the A.T.F. Co., both partners retiring from business. A brief, highly successful career. Its specimen books record its leadership in type faces.

Central Type Foundry, March 1889 (849) Price List of Type and Printing
Material. Central Type Foundry, Manufacturers of the celebrated
Copper Alloy Type. St. Louis, 1889 .... $ 4.75
Boards, lge. 8vo. pp.314; complete; good condition.

Central Type Foundry, 1893 (850) Specimens of Brass Types, Rules,
Borders and Ornaments for Bookbinders, 1893 .... 1.25
Cloth, pp.32; good condition.

Cincinnati Type Foundry (629.63) Specimens of Printing Types, cast
and for sale by the C. T. F., corner of Vine and Longworth Sts.,
L.T. Wells, agent. Cincinnati, 1856 .... 14.00
Boards, cover loose, lge 4to, pp.230, 2pp. paper and ink advertisements for other concerns; complete; contents in good condition.
    The C. T. F. was established by Oliver and Horace Wells in 1817,
the earliest in the territory west of Philadelphia. (In some of its
eighteen type specimen books 1820 is given as the date of its origin).
Wells had an immense and steadily growing market in the west and along
the Mississippi, and soon began the manufacture of printing machinery,
equipments and tools. In 1830 the business was incorporated, the Wells'
remaining in control until Charles Wells died in 1885. At the time of
the Civil War this was the leading foundry in the west. Henry Barth, the
inventor of the Barth automatic type casting machine, which quickly
superceded the Bruce type casting machine, succeeded Charles Wells in the
control. In 1892 he merged the business with the A.T.F. Co. These are
the dates of the specimen books known to us: 1834, 1844, 1851, 1852,
1853, 1856, 1857, 1860, 1862, 1864, 1874, 1876, 1880, 1882, 1888, 1893.

Cincinnati Type Foundry (852). The Cincinnati Type Foundry and Printing
Machine Works. Charles Wells, secretary. Cincinnati, 1862 .... 12.00
Cloth, lge. 4to $\frac{3}{4}$ in. thick; sound condition; complete. All
the type faces made by this foundry since 1817 are exhibited.

Cincinnati Type Foundry (629.64) The Specimen Book of the Cincinnati
Type Foundry 1874 .... 3.00
Half leather and cloth, lge. 4to. 1 in. thick; sound, but scuffed
and finger marked, a few pages slightly cut, hence low price.

Cincinnati Type Foundry (853) Thirteenth Specimen Book from the
Cincinnati Type Foundry. Established 1817. Cincinnati: 201
Vine Street and 7-17 Longworth Street, 1880 .... 8.00
Cloth, lge. 4to. pp. xxviii (price list of machinery and other
equipments), 158 (type specimens); sound, complete, contents in
good condition.

Cincinnati Type Foundry (854) The Sixteenth Specimen Book and
Catalogue of Machinery, from the C.T.F. Compact edition.
Cincinnati 1885 ....6.25
Cloth, 8 vo. pp.284, good condition, complete. Has all the famous
borders (pp. 920-1036); card ornaments, head bands and decorative
material, original with this foundry. An attractive book.

Cincinnati Type Foundry (629.65) The Seventeenth Book of Specimens, from the C.T.F. Compact edition. Cincinnati, 1888 .... $ 4.50
Cloth, 8 vo. pp.xxxi (machinery made by C.T.F.), 182 (type specimens), 96 (cuts), 72 (selection of type faces type foundries); complete; sound and in good condition.

Cincinnati Type Foundry (856). Same book as above - (The Seventeenth) - minus 72 pages of selections of type faces from other type foundries. Cincinnati, 1888 .... 3.25
Cloth, 8 vo; sound and in good condition.

Cincinnati Type Foundry (858). Condensed Specimen Book from the C. T.F. Established 1817. Compact edition. Cincinnati,1893..... 2.75
Limp cloth, 8 vo. pp.188, xiv; complete and in good condition.

Cincinnati Type Foundry (860) The Eighteenth Book of Specimens from the C.T.F. Established in 1817. Compact edition. Cincinnati, 1893 .... 4.50
Cloth, 8 vo. pp.xxxii, 1a-24a, 1-88, 89c - 180c, 89-103 (specimens of German type faces), 104-188, 1-96 (original borders, and decorative material, cuts). This book was printed in Cincinnati though issued by the A.T.F. Co. in 1893. It contains all that was best of the manufactures of the C.T.F. before the plant moved to Jersey City. Where the paginations are followed by the letters a and c, the pages show type faces of other branches of the A.T.F. Co. many of them very beautiful; complete and in good condition,

Boston Type Foundry (823). First letter foundry in New England, Established 1817. Condensed Specimen Book from the B.T.F. John K. Rogers & Co., proprietors, Boston, 1860 ....5.00
Cloth, covers loose but not detached; 4to, $\frac{1}{2}$ in. thick; complete; contains all the type faces made by the B.T.F. since 1817, some quite fanciful.

Cleveland Type Foundry (863) Catalogue (of printers' supplies) and Book of Specimens from the C.T.F. the H.H. Thorp Mfg. Co., 147 St. Clair Street, Cleveland, O., circa 1880 ....4.50
This is the first specimen book of this type foundry. While it has no date, the copy on our shelves has on the fly leaf this note, written by Mr. F. B. Berry who was the secretary and manager of the C.T.F. during its entire career (1879-1892); "This is the first specimen book issued by the C.T.F. printed in 1880. It contains on p.139 the first display type of original design cast by this foundry (Typographic Combination)". This was followed by a number of type faces, shown in subsequent books, of ingenious original character. Other specimen books were issued in 1883,1885,1890,1891,1895. This foundry also made Gordon Printing Presses.

Cleveland Type Foundry (865). Catalogue and Price List of Type and Material, C.T.F., Cleveland, O., 1893 ....4.50
Cloth, 8 vo. pp.408; complete and in good condition. Contains the most extraordinary type faces every made in the U.S.

Cleveland Type Foundry (864) Catalogue and Book of Specimens of Type Faces and Printing Material and Machinery. Cleveland, O., 1895 ....5.00
Cloth, 8vo., pp.454; complete and in good condition.
Contains specimens of all the type faces made by the C.T.F. with the addition of a few type faces made elsewhere. This book was printed in Cleveland, but issued by the new owners, the A.T.F. Co.

Conner Type Foundry (629.66). Conner's United States Type Foundry. A
    miniature Specimen of Printing Types and Ornaments, from the
    Type and Stereotype Foundry of James Conner & Son, Franklin
    Buildings, corner Nassau and Ann Streets, New York, 1841........$40.00
    Half leather and boards, med. 8 vo. $1\frac{1}{4}$ ins. complete; sound
and in good condition; an attractive book, contents perfectly clean;
covers scuffed.

    James Conner introduced stereotyping in Boston, as one of the
foremen of the Boston Type Founders Co. He was a printer by trade.
Returning to New York in 1827 he stereotyped, printed and published
several books accepted as classics, including an edition of the Holy
Bible. He printed his own imprint on a limited number of these books,
and on a larger number printed the imprint of booksellers who would
buy a sufficient quantity. In this enterprise he prospered. In 1829
he entered the type making industry, with a series of lightface
romans and italics, designed and cut by David Bruce, Jr., who sub-
sequently invented the first practicable type casting machine. After he
died in 1861 his sons and grandsons carried on the business, until it
was sold in 1892 to the A.T.F. Co. In 1861 the C.T.F. was even more
extensive than those of White and of Bruce. Specimens on our shelves
of this foundry are: 1829 (broadside), 1834 (Conner & Cooke), 1836,
1837, circa 1841, n.d. (James Conner & Son, William), 1841, 1850, 1852,
1855, 1859, 1860, 1870, 1885 (issued in two sections), 1888, 1891.

Conner Type Foundry (629.70). Specimens of Printing Types, plain and
    ornamental Rules, Borders, Ornaments, etc., from the United
    States Type Foundry, James Conner & Sons. 28-32 Centre Street,
    New York, n.d. circa 1860 .... 27.50
    The preface is signed by James Conner & Sons, with the separate
signatures of James Conner and two sons, Wm. Crawford Conner and James
Madison Conner. This book was the first issued from Centre Street,
most of it while James Conner was alive. The title page was printed
after J.C. died, the firm name changing after that event.
    Half leather and cloth, royal 4to. $1\frac{1}{2}$ ins., cover loose but not
broken; scuffed, contents complete; rare; last ten pages consist of
an interesting catalogue of printing machinery and tools made by
Taylor, Ruggles, Montague, Hawks, and Hoe. Well worth rebinding.

Conner Type Foundry (629.69) Specimens of plain and ornamental print-
    ing Types, Rules, Dashes and Ornaments, cast at the United States
    Type Foundry of James Conner's Sons, New York, Nos. 28-32 Centre
    Street, New York, n.d. circa 1870 ....30.00
    Half leather and cloth, sound condition; lge. folio; $2\frac{1}{2}$ ins.
pp.1-113 at end show interesting collection of cuts; all specimens
printed on one side only; contents complete and in excellent condition. At this date Conner's was the leading type foundry in New York.
In this book is the first showing in New York of old style roman and
italic and Hebrew types.

Conner Type Foundry (870). Specimens of Plain and Ornamental types,
    cast by the United States Type Foundry of James Conner's Sons,
    New York, Nos. 28-32 Centre Street, circa 1876 .... 25.00
    Half leather and cloth, covers loose; lge. folio, $2\frac{1}{4}$ ins. ;
full page mezzotint wood cut of the Conner Foundry as frontispiece;
preface signed by three sons, the addition being, E.S. Conner; at
end pp.1-124 of cuts; contents complete and in good condition. Well
worth rebinding.

Conner Type Foundry (629.67). Abridged Specimens of Printing Types,
Brass Rules, Electrotypes (Cuts) and Revised Catalogue of
Printing Materials, James Conner's Sons, New York: the United
States Type Foundry, 1888 ....$5.50
Cloth, royal 4to. 1 in., sound; contents complete and in good
condition.

Conner Type Foundry (874). Ornamental Type and Borders manufactured
by James Conner's Sons (United States Type Foundry); type
founders, Centre, Reade and Duane Sts., New York, 1886.......... 5.50
Paper (title on cover), royal 4to 1 in. ; complete and in
excellent condition; a beautiful collection of combination
borders many of them for printing in two or more colors, several
shown in their colors; the best printed of all the Conner specimen
This is the third section of a larger book planned but not completed,
as we learn from the preface of the second section (CC-4-4 on our shelves
of which we have no duplicate). Well worth rebinding.

Crescent Type Foundry (877). Specimens of Type, Borders and Ornaments
Brass Rule, etc., Price List of Printers' Machinery and
Materials. Crescent Type Foundry. Chicago: 346 Dearborn Street,
1899 .... 2.50
Stamped cloth, sound, scuffed; 8 vo. pp.673; contents complete
and in good condition; a well printed book; interesting contents;
view of premises as a frontispiece.

Dickinson Type Foundry (878) Commenced in 1840. Specimens of Types
for Newspaper Printing, Newspaper Ornaments, Brass Rules, etc.,
from the foundry of Phelps and Dalton, No. 52 Washington Street,
Boston, Mass., July 1855 .... 4.75
Boards, cloth back, sound; med. 4to, $\frac{1}{4}$ ins.; contents well printed
and complete.
In 1842 Samuel Nelson Dickinson was the best and most enterprising
printer in the U.S. In that year he added typemaking to his business,
issuing an attractive type specimen book at 52 Washington Street,
Boston. He died in 1848. His typefounding business was bought by Phelps
& Dalton, two expert heads of departments in the Boston Type Foundry.
Although P & D were both dead, the business was carried on as P., D.
& Co. until 1889. In 1890 the D.T.F. came under the control of the
distinguished Joseph Warren Phinney, who had previously been manager of
it for several years. At all time the D.T.F. was, while not the most
extensive, the most distinguished type foundry in New England. In 1892
it was bought by the A.T.F. Co. In 1933 J.W.Phinney resigned as manager,
but is still a director and vice-president. Specimen books of this foundry
were issued in 1842, 1843, 1846 (4-page broadside), 1847, 1849 (demy broadside, showing 68 fonts of types), 1859, 1867, 1868, 1872, 1878, 1883,
1888, 1890, 1892 (combination of D.T.F. and Boston Type Foundry specimens,
issued by the A.T.F. Co.)

Dickinson Type Foundry (879) The Minor Specimen Book of the D.T. F.
Phelps & Dalton, Boston, Mass., 1859 .... 3.75
Boards, loose, scuffed, royal 4to. $\frac{3}{4}$ ins. ; contents complete
and in good condition; rare; covers well worth repairing.

Dickinson Type Foundry (880) The Minor Specimen Book of the D.T.F.
Comprising Plain and Ornamental Types, Brass Rules, Electrotype
Cuts, etc. Phelps, Dalton & Co., proprietors, Boston 1867 ....$4.50
Rebound, cloth, leather back, sound;royal 4to, $\frac{1}{2}$ in.; contents
complete and in good condition.

Dickinson Type Foundry (882) General Book of Specimens, showing Plain
and Ornamental Type, Brass Rule, Electrotypes, etc. Boston,
Phelps, Dalton & Company, proprietors, 1879 ....6.50
Half leather and cloth, 4to (12 x 10$\frac{1}{4}$), pp.363, printed on one
side only; covers loose, back missing; contents complete and in good
condition; well worth rebinding. The firm in 1879 was Pierce,
Phemister and Converse.

Dickinson Type Foundry (883). Specimens of Printing Types, Rules, Cuts,
and Letterpress Printing Material. Phelps, Dalton & Co. Boston,
236 Washington Street, 1883 ....6.50
Cloth, covers loose but not detached; 4to., pp.251; contents
complete and in good condition; where type faces of other foundries
are exhibited the names of the originating foundries are printed;
an up-to-date (1883) specimen book.

Dickinson Type Foundry (887). Point System Specimen Book. Specimens
of Printing Types, Rules Cuts, Printing Material. Boston:
D.T.F. 150 Congress Street, 1900 ....8.00
Cloth, covers loose but not detached; 4to, pp.248; contents
complete and in good condition; several type faces of great merit
shown for the first time; last book issued by the D.T.F.

Dickinson Type Foundry (889) Point Specimen Book, Specimens of
Printing Types, Rules, Cuts, Printing Materials. Our
Collective Specimen Book. Boston, n.d., circa 1893 ....6.50
As a result of the consolidation of the Boston and
Dickinson type foundries in 1892 this collective book of both
type foundries was issued, omitting earlier type faces which were,
at the time, deemed obsolete, and adding a selection from other
foundries operated by the A.T.F. Co. A well arranged and well
printed book. Rare and desirable.
Cloth, sound condition, 4to.,pp.48 (Machinery and printing
materials, illus.) 53-285 (products of the Boston and Central
foundries), 287-396 (products of the D.T.F.), 397-439 (Selection
of products of other A.T.F. Co. foundries.

Farmer, Little & Co. (892). White's Type Foundry, Established 1810.
Specimens of printing types from F. L. & Co., Nos. 63 and 65
Beekman Street, New York, 1862 ....4.00
Cloth, covers loose, needs rebinding; 4to, $\frac{3}{4}$ ins.; contents
complete; show marks of handling; specimen pages have various imprints:
Chas. T. White & Co. , Chicago Type Foundry; White Type Foundry,
and F. L. & Co.
Andrew Little, John Bentley, and A.D. Farmer were employees of
Chas. T. White, type founder (see White in this list). They acquired
the foundry in 1862, and continued it until 1892, in which year Little
and Bentley retired, leaving Farmer sole owner. He died in 1895 succeeded by his son, who sold the foundry to the A.T.F. Co. in 1899. Specimen
books were issued by the F., L., & Co. partnership in 1862, 1865, 1867,

1868, 1873, 1874, 1877, 1878, 1880, 1882, 1885, 1887, 1892, 1893, 1895, 1897, 1899, 1900 (the last by the A.T.F. Co. under the name of A.D. Farmer & Son Type Founding Co.)

Farmer, Little & Co. (894). Specimens of Printing Types, Ornaments, Borders, etc., from the type foundry and printers' warehouse of F.L. & Co. Established 1810. New York, 1880 .... $6.00
    Cloth, leather back, front cover detached; royal 4to, $1\frac{3}{4}$ ins. ; specimens printed on one side only,

Farmer, Little & Co. (629.72) Type Foundry and Printers' Warehouse Established in 1804. The Specimen Book of Types from F.L. & Co. Rules, Cuts, Borders, etc. New York, 1885 .... 7.50
    Cloth, leather back, covers loose, require repairing or rebinding; super royal 4to, pp.ccxxlv, 185. An interesting, well edited and well printed book; worthy of repairing or rebinding.

Farmer, Little & Co. (896). The reduced Price List and latest Specimens of Printing Types, etc., in an abridged form, cast by F.L. & Co., New York, 1882. With supplement, pp.32, of new type faces since 1882. Cover stamped 1885 .... 6.50
    Cloth, 8vo. in excellent condition, pp.192 and 32.

Farmer, Little & Co. (897). Selected Type Faces from the foundry of F. L. & Co. Established 1804. New York, 1889 .... 3.00
    Boards, demy 8vo. pp.144; excellent condition.

Farmer, Little & Co. (898) Specimens from the type foundry of F.L. & Co., including book, newspaper and jobbing type, plain and ornamental brass rules, complete price list, etc. New York, 1892 .... 2.75
    Cloth, limp, medium 8vo. pp.304; covers sound; contents complete, one signature loose; worth repairing.

Farmer, A.D. & Sons Co. (899) Established 1804. Abridged Specimen Book, Type, Borders, Brass Rules, Ornaments and Price List of Printing Machinery, Furniture, Fixtures and Material. A. D. Farmer & Son Type Founding Co., Chicago, 163-165 fifth Avenue, 1899.. 3.00
    Cloth, sound condition, 8 x $5\frac{1}{2}$ ins. pp. 400. Printed and issued by the Chicago selling house of Farmer.

Farmer, A.D. & Son Co. (629.73) Title page: Typographic Specimens, Illustrated Catalogue. September 1900. Stamped on front cover; Book of Specimens, Type. A.D. Farmer & Son Type Founding Co., 63-65 Beekman Street, New York; on back cover; Old New York Type Foundry. Established 1804................ 4.25
    Cloth, excellent condition, demy 8 vo. pp.596

Franklin Type Foundry (904) The Pocket Book of Specimens. Cincinnati F.T.F. No. 168 Vine St. n.d. (circa 1878) 20.00
    This is the second book issued by the F.T.F. its first book was issued in 1871 (a lge. 4to, 2 ins. thick, elegantly printed on one side of the paper only, in Cincinnati, by the Western Methodist Book Concern). This item is also exceptionally well printed. It is

very rare. It was probably printed between the years 1876 and 1878,
four supplements meanwhile being issued, all dated and included at end
of book, but paged consecutively with the preceding page. This item is
well bound in cloth, in sound condition, 8 x 5 ins., pp.246, viii.

The Franklin Type Foundry was established at the end of the
Civil War as a branch of the foundry of L. Johnson & Co., Philadelphia
(see Johnson T.F. below). The branch was operated by Robert Allison,
Chas. H. Smith and H. L. Johnson, the two last named being relatives
of the partners in L.J. & Co. In 1867 these three employees purchased
the Cincinnati business. In 1883 H.L. Johnson retired. The business,
which had prospered, was continued by A. and S. until 1892, when it was
merged with the American Type Founders Co., of which Allison was the
first president. Specimen books were issued by the F.T.F. in 1871,
circa 1878, 1880, 1883, 1885, 1888, 1890 and several small supplements.
All its specimens were printed in successful emulation with MacKellar,
Smiths & Jordan's books.

Franklin Type Foundry (905) Convenient Book of Specimens. F.T.F.
    Cincinnati, Allison & Smith, 168 Vine Street, 1890 ....$9.50
    Cloth, excellent condition, medium 8vo. pp.xxiv, 425; rare.

Gilchrist, A.S.(906) Book of Specimens of Printing Types, Cuts,
    Ornaments, etc., cast at the Knickerbocker Type Foundry of
    A.S.G. Albany, N.Y., 75 State St., near North Pearl, 1857............10.00
    Cloth, leather back, sound condition; royal 4to 3/8 in.
    The first type foundry in Albany began in 1829. At one time
Albany had three type foundries.

Hagar Type Foundry (629.74) Specimens of Printing Types, Ornaments
    Borders, etc., from the Type Foundry of Wm. Hagar, Jr. & Co.,
    New York, 38 Gold Street, 1858 .... 6.00
    Cloth loose, med. royal, $\frac{3}{4}$ ins. Has insert, p.6 of types for
printing in colors, issued by W. & H. Hagar.
    William Hagar was an employee of Elihu White, who began
typefounding in New York in 1810. In 1826 a type specimen book
was issued by William Hagar & Co., No.223 Pearl and 20 Gold Streets,
N.Y. In 1854 the firm name was W. and H. Hagar (a brother), 38 Gold Street.
In 1858 the firm name was Wm Hagar Jr. & Co., 38 Gold Street. In
1866 to 1886 the firm name was Hagar & Co., at 38 Gold Street. The
foundry was dispersed at auction in 1887. Specimen books were issued
in 1826, 1831, 1841, 1850, 1854(2), 1860(2), 1860(2), 1866, 1873, 1886.
In the two latter books it is claimed that the Hagar foundry was established in 1818, which is doubtful.

Hagar Type Foundry (629.75) Specimens (abridged) of Printing Types,
    Ornaments, Borders, etc., from the Type Foundry and Printers'
    Emporium of Hagar & Co. Established in 1818. New York: 38 Gold
    Street, 1866 .... 6.00
    Cloth, sound, scuffed, 4to, $11\frac{3}{4}$ x $9\frac{1}{2}$ x $\frac{1}{2}$ ins.

Hamilton Mfg. Co., (919) Specimens of Wood Type, Ornaments, etc., made
    by the H.M. Co. Seventeenth Edition. Two Rivers, Wis., 1901 .... 2.25
    Paper covers, perfect condition; 13 x 10 x $\frac{1}{2}$ ins. Full-page
picture of factories as frontispiece.

Hansen Type Foundry (911). Specimen Book of Type and Printing Material
manufactured by H. C. Hansen, type founder, 190-192 Congress
Street, Boston, Mass., n.d. circa 1903 ....$2.00
Cloth, sound; fcap 4to. pp.248.

Hansen Type Foundry (912) Hansen's BrassRules. Greatest variety and
most exclusive designs ever produced. Boston: H. C. Hansen
Type Foundry, 190-192 Congress St., n.d. (circa 1906) 2.25
Paper, 4to, pp.80. This is the most complete specimen book
of everything in brass and steel rules and spacing material ever
printed in the U.S. Perfect condition. Full page portrait of H.C.
Hansen and views of his establishment. Established in 1872.

Illinois Type Foundry (914) First Specimen of the I.T.F. Co. For
additional specimens after this date, see Supplement at end of
this book. Chicago, No. 61 and 63 West Lake Street, April 1873...... 4.25
Cloth, royal 8vo. pp.xix, 168; excellent condition; This was
a branch of the Bruce Foundry of N.Y. In addition to type faces made
locally, it contains specimens of a larger number of the quaint type
faces originated at the Bruce Foundry. Other specimen books were
issued in 1883, 1887.

Inland Type Foundry (915). Specimen Book and Catalog. A Price List of
Printers Supplies, showing types and Rules in which are embodied
all the latest ideas that enable the Printer to produce Superior
Work in a most Economical Manner; among which Betterments may be
especially mentioned the casting of types on Standard Line
(invented by the I.T.F.) and Unit Sets. St. Louis, Inland Type
Foundry, February 1897 ....5.00
Cloth on stiff boards, sound; contents clean and complete;
crown 8vo, pp.239. All editions of this item have the same
format and title page. They differ only in the number of pages,
which increase as new specimens of types are added. All I.T.F.
specimen books have careful explanations of their standard line
and unit set (width) systems, which made this foundry famous.
Although this foundry had a career of only 17 years, it must ever
be regarded as extraordinarily important in the history of typemaking.
It may safely be predicted that its specimen books will be highly regarded as collector's items in the future, whatever may happen to the
industry. This foundry's first specimen book, issued in 1895, announced
a great improvement in typemaking -- the Standard Lining System -- an
entirely novel idea, first utilized by the I.T.F. which gave to the type
faces made by it a superiority so obvious that in a few years all American
type foundries were compelled to adopt the system and, at great expense,
to re-align all their salable type faces. Types not re-aligned are now
known as Old Line type faces and are in the obsolete class. In 1912
the I.T.F. was merged with the A.T.F. Co., and its plant moved to
Jersey City. Before the merger the I.T.F. issued more than a score
of specimen books. From 1897 to 1902, all the books were dated on
the title pages, Feb. 1897, while the dates of issue of each edition
were stamped on the covers, Therefore, it will not be necessary here
to repeat the rather lengthy title page which appears precisely the
same in all editions. Books on our shelves issued by the I.T.F.:
1895 (2), 1897 (2), 1899 (2), 1901 (2), 1902, 1903, 1906, 1907, 1910(2),
1912.

Inland Type Foundry (916). Issued and dated Feb. 1897; pp.364, 98 of
     which contain an illus. catalogue of printing machinery and
     materials (see paragraph above) ....$ 6.50
------(917) Issued June 1899; title page dated Feb. 1897; pp.366,
     all type specimens, no catalogue of other supplies........... 6.50
------(918) Issued Dec. 1899; title page dated Feb. 1897; pp.434.... 6.75
------(920) Issued March 1901; pp.464, includes pp.82 of an Illus.
     catalogue of printing machinery and supplies.................. 7.00
------(921) Issued May 1902; pp.470, includes pp. of an illus.
     catalogue of printing machinery and supplies 7.25

Inland Type Foundry (922) Specimen Book and Catalogue; a Price
     List of Printers' Supplies, Type, Rules and Accessories of the
     very latest designs, which facilitate the economical production
     of superior printing. A Notable Improvement is the casting of
     all Types on Standard Line and Unit Sets. Inland Type Foundry,
     St. Louis, New York and Chicago, September 1907 ....12.50
     Cloth, all in good condition and complete; med. 8vo.;
pp.243, devoted entirely to types and decorative material.

Inland Type Foundry (923) Title page the same as for item 922.
     Issued September 1910 ....13.50
     Cloth, all in good condition and complete; med. 8vo., pp.308
(16 pp. at end has price list of printing materials)

Inland Type Foundry (924) (A loose-leaf Specimen Book). Specimen Book
     and Catalogue. A Price List of Printers' Supplies, showing Types
     and Rules, in which are embodied all the latest ideas that enable
     the Printer to produce superior work in a most economical manner;
     among which betterments may be mentioned the casting of Type on
     Standard Line and Unit Set. Inland Type Foundry, St. Louis,
     New York and Chicago. June 1906 ....16.00
     Cloth loose leaf binder, royal 4to., about 300 pages devoted
to type faces and 42 pages to an illus. Price List of Machinery
and Supplies. This book exhibits all the products of the I.T.F.
until its close in 1912-- the most interesting collection of this
foundry's product, with a careful explanation of Standard Lining
and Unit Set Systems and a fine view of the building built for and
owned by this company.

Johnson Type Foundry (629.78) Specimen of Printing Types and
     Ornaments, cast by L. Johnson, successor to Johnson & Smith,
     No. 6 George Street, Philadelphia, 1844......................20.00
     Half leather, intact but worn, med. 8vo. 3 in., contents
complete and in good condition.
     This foundry was established by Binney & Ronaldson in 1796,
and was continued by James Ronaldson and Richard Ronaldson until
1833, in which year it was purchased by Johnson & Smith, a partnership which continued until 1843, Smith withdrawing, Johnson continuing as sole owner until 1845, when MacKellar and Smith formed,
with Johnson, the firm of Johnson & Co. which continued until 1867,
though Johnson died in 1860. In 1867 the firm of MacKellar, Smiths,
& Jordan was formed, continuing until 1892. They were succeeded by
the A.T.F. Co. (See Binny & Ronaldson and MacKellar, Smiths & Jordan).

Duplicates

Johnson Type Foundry (926) Minor Book of Specimens of Printing Types
    cast at the foundry of L. Johnson & Co. (Lawrence Johnson,
    Thomas MacKellar, J. F. Smith) Established by Binny & Ronaldson
    in 1796, Philadelphia; No. 6 Sansom Street near the Statehouse,
    1853 ....$4.50
        Cloth, sound, somewhat discolored, royal 4to., pp.ii, 74,
several pages cut, hence the low price; very interesting book,
nevertheless, to students.

Kansas City Type Foundry (930) Price List of Printing Material,
    K.C.T.F., established 1872, J.T. Reton & Son, Prop's. 606
    Broadway, Kansas City, Mo., Jan. 1, 1887 ....3.50
        Limp imitation leather, sound demy 8vo. pp.288; contents
complete and in good condition. This is the fifth specimen of this
foundry; another book was issued later, circa 1889. In 1892 the
foundry was bought by the A.T.F. Co. and the plant moved to another
city. Very rare.

Keystone Type Foundry (931) Specimen Book of Type, made from
    nickel-alloy metal by the K.T.F.; also containing a catalogue
    of Printers' Supplies. For sale at the foundry, 734-740 Sansome
    Street, Philadelphia, 1899.. 3.25
        Limp leather, worn but intact, 8vo. pp.405 with addendum
pp.32.
        This foundry was established in 1888. It produced many
original type designs. It was sold to the A.T.F. Co. in 1919.

Keystone Type Foundry (932) Specimen Book of Type Faces, showing
    the latest and best products of a Modern Type Foundry, all of
    which are made of Nickel-Alloy Type Metal. Philadelphia:
    corner Eighth and Sansom Streets, 1901 .... 5.00
        Cloth, 8vo. sound; contents complete and in good condition;
pp.xxxii, A 1-16, B 1-16, C 1-16, 17-128 (129-163); pp.227 in all.

Keystone Type Foundry (934) Abridged Specimen Book of Types--and
    Catalogue of General Supplies, K.T.F., Philadelphia, inventors
    and sole makers of nickel-alloy type. Issued February 1905......... 6.00
        Cloth, sound, slightly soiled, demy 8vo. pp.488; contents
complete, in good condition.

Keystone Type Foundry (935) Abridged Specimen Book. Nickel-
    Alloy Types on Universal Line, comprising a Price List of
    Types, Borders, Leads and Slugs, Brass Rule...and General
    Supplies for Printers. K.T.F. Philadelphia, September 1906...........7.50
        Cloth, sound, slightly soiled, demy 8vo. pp.623; contents
complete; in good condition.

Keystone Type Foundry (936) Catalogue and Specimen Book. Keystone
    Products, consisting of Type, Material, Furniture. Complete
    Line of Miscellaneous Supplies for Printers and Publishers.
    Machinery and Wood Goods (Philadelphia); Keystone Type
    Foundry, n.d. (1915) 17.50
        Cloth, sound, med. 4to., pp.649. Contents complete and in
good condition. Two frontispieces have pictures of premises
occupied by its six houses, the main office and foundry in
Philadelphia, the branch houses in Chicago, New York, Detroit,

Atlanta and San Francisco. This book was issued at the height of
the prosperity of this foundry, and is its last complete issue.
Subsequent issues were little more than pamphlets, which served
their purpose, until the foundry was purchased by the A.T.F. Co.
The best Keystone book. It was issued for the Chicago house.

Lothian Type Foundry (937) Specimen of Printing Types, by George B.
    Lothian, No.42 Spruce St. near Gold St., New York, 1841.........$9.50
    Boards, leather, sound, mod. 8vo. ½ in.; contents complete
and in good condition; rare.
    George B. Lothian was a son of Dr. Robert Lothian, an eminent
scholar-typefounder who came to New York from Scotland in 1806, with
the equipments for a type foundry, which he conducted unsuccessfully
until he sold the foundry to Binny & Ronaldson in 1810. George B.
Lothian was a masterly type founder, a skillful punch cutter, un-
excelled in his time, with a background of training in Scotland and
employment in the best type foundries in the U.S. In 1823 he established a type foundry in New York City, issuing his first
specimen book in 1832, his second book in 1841. He died in 1850.
His foundry was acquired from his executors by Cortelyou & Giffing.
The contents of the book here offered were the work of his own hands
as punch cutter and exhibit his mastery of that art.

Lindsay Type Foundry (939) Issued without title page -- title on
    cover: Specimens of Printing Types made by the L. T. F., 75
    Fulton St., New York, n. d. circa 1891 ....5.00
    Cloth, 12 x 9½ x 3¾ in., complete and in excellent condition;
rare.
    Four Lindsays came from Scotland in 1852. They were exception-
ally good type founders. Robert and John began type founding in
1852; in 1856 a brother, Alex. W., joined the firm; soon Alex. W.
separated from his brothers and established an opposition foundry
which continued to 1892, when it was sold to the A.T.F. Co. John
Lindsay died, and the first Lindsay Foundry was continued by Robert
until 1903. In 1866 a fourth brother, James, became a partner in
the Bruce Type Foundry. The book here offered was issued by Robert.

MacKellar, Smiths & Jordan Co. (629.84) Seventeenth Specimen Book.
    Printers' Handy Book of Type Specimens, Borders, Cuts, Rules,
    etc., made by the MacKellar, Smiths & Jordan Co. Offices and
    foundry, 606-614 Sansom Street, Philadelphia. June 1890 ....47.50
    Half morocco, mod. 4to, pp.525; stout, scuffed, contents
complete and in good condition; beautifully printed.
    This firm was successor to Binny & Ronaldson (1796-1815), the
Ronaldsons (1815-1833), Johnson & Smith (1833-1843), Lawrence
Johnson (1843-1845), Johnson & Co. (1845-1867), MacKellar, Smiths
& Jordan (1867-1892), becoming the parent foundry of the American
Type Founders Co. in the latter year. The foundry is now in
Jersey City. (See notes of these various partnerships under the
firm names).
    When in 1867 Thomas MacKellar became the controlling influence
in the firm, he, in a few years, made it the most eminent foundry
in the world, both in the artistic quality and volume of its products.

He gave to American type making a leadership that has been maintained until the present time. Thomas MacKellar gave his personal attention to the editing and printing of the type specimen books issued by his firm. From 1867 to 1890 he was not only the author of the texts, but also the composer of the lines of types -- a composer in two senses of that word, -- by which his types were advertised. These lines are famous for their appropriateness and wit and humor. The books thus edited by him are the only type specimen books which may be read with pleasure! We regret that in this list only one of the books having MacKellar characteristics is offered. It is the item immediately above (629.84), issued in 1890, when the most illustrious of American type founders was seventy-eight years of age, nine years before the year of his death in 1899. Among the initiate these MacKellar classics are, among type specimen books, now most in demand -- they are already collector's items, more treasured than any other American type specimen books, hence their absence from this list. (Here are examples of the MacKellar specimen texts (p.292 of item 629.84: "Domisomi Quickstep, Grace in her Step and Heaven in hereEye"; and "Life Dream: Dimple and Wrinkle"; and "Coatings: Lady's Patent Blushes".)

Apart from the editing, the type lines were displayed most effectively; the printing, as exemplified by our 629.84 is the most perfect done in type specimen books anywhere -- beyond criticism; In the item here offered there are 99 pages of woodcut designs for use on printing for all occasions and purposes -- more than 1200 in all. These were all engraved by Beiler, an engraver constantly engaged by MacKellar. Until a quarter century ago all type foundries included cuts in their specimen books. It is true that every electro-type cut shown in MacKellar's specimen books were made from original wood engravings of great merit, which, in addition to satisfying the printers, were also a source of supply to competing type founders, few of whom ever produced an original design. Another merit of item 629.84 is that the originality of the Mackellar type faces is attested by printing the dates of the patents with each specimen showing. The item 629.84 is a masterpiece. Fortunate will be the future possessor.

MacKellar, Smiths & Jordan Co. (945) New and Original Old Style Types. Philadelphia, n.d. (circa 1886) ....$ 1.25
    Cloth, demy 4to., pp.16; excellent condition; composition and presswork in two colors, perfect. This is a specimen of the Ronaldson series. The text used is the opening of a biography of James Ronaldson written by Dr. Thomas MacKellar, with on alternate pages of poetry written by MacKellar.

MacKellar, Smiths & Jordan Co. (629.83) Compact Book, eighteenth Specimen Book. Specimens of Printing Types, made by the MacKellar Smiths & Jordan Co., type founders and electrotypers. Nos.606-614 Sansom St., Philadelphia, June 1888 .... 5.00
    Cloth, med. 8vo. pp.464; covers loose, but not detached; contents admirably represent the products of the leading type foundry of the world; slightly soiled by handling.

Mechanics Type Foundry (949) Specimen Book of Printing Types, Borders, Cuts, Rules, etc., M.T.F. (Creswell, Wanner & Co.) Chicago: Office and Foundry, 172 and 174 South Clark Street, 1880 .... 2.25
    Cloth, quarto, 5/8 ins., sound, scuffed; contents complete, except that cuts of two printing presses have been neatly excised.

This foundry began in 1872; its name was changed to the Union Type
Foundry in 1883. In 1893 it was sold to the A.T.F. Co.

Marder, Luse & Co.(953) Specimens of Printing Types, Borders and
    Brass Rule, furnished by the Chicago Type Foundry, M.L.&Co.
    Chicago, n.d. (circa 1870) $5.00
        Cloth, royal 4to.$\frac{1}{4}$in., covers loose, contents complete
and in good condition.
        This was the first type foundry in Chicago. It was established
as a branch of C.T. White & Co., New York City, in 1855. A specimen
book was issued by the Chicago house in 1862. It was printed in New
York. The foundry was sold in 1863 to D. Scofield & Co.; in 1864 the
owners were Scofield, Marder and Collins; in 1869 the owners were
Marder, Luse & Co. For many years it was the leading type foundry
west of the Ohio. The item offered above was the first type
specimen book printed in Chicago, the only one before the Chicago
fire. It is a creditable production, well worth rebinding. In
1881 this foundry had the distinction of being the first to cast
type on point bodies on the principle invented by Fournier in
France in 1734. All foundries in English speaking countries
followed the example of the Chicago Type Foundry, as it was the
principal improvement made in type founding since the invention
of printing types.

Marder, Luse & Co. (629.86) Price List and Printer's Purchasing Guide
    issued by M.L. & Co., Chicago type Foundry, 139-141 Munroe
    Street, April 1, 1881 ....3.50
        Paper, 6$\frac{1}{2}$ x 4, pp.272; covers in bad condition; contents
complete and exceedingly interesting and important. This has the
first description of the "American System of Interchangeable Type
Bodies" on 3 pages. So new was this system when this book was
issued that none of the sizes of types shown in this book are
designated by points. There is an excellent illus. description
of type making, 5 pages. Although the covers are shabby, this rare
book deserves to be preserved on account of its historical importance.

Marder, Luse & Co. (951) Chicago Type Foundry. Price List and
    Printer's Purchasing Guide, showing Printing Type manufactured
    by Marder, Luse & Co. 139-141 Munroe Street, Chicago, 1890........4.50
        Boards, f cap, 8vo. pp.554; in good condition; an up-to-date
book in 1890.

Marder, Luse & Co. (952) Specimen Book of Printing Types, Borders,
    Brass Rule, etc., manufactured by M.L.& Co. type founders,
    Chicago and San Francisco, 1881 ....5.25
        Cloth, med. 4to. 5/8 ins. sound but scuffed; contents complete
and in good condition; rare and of historical interest; well worth
preserving.
        This book was printed in 1880, the year before the point system
of interchangeable type bodies was offered for sale. This important
improvement is explained here, with diagrams, but before renaming of
the sizes was put into effect - the old names, which are now obsolete
were retained. Every item shown in this book, made in casting machines,
were of this foundry's manufacture. Three pages are devoted to a good
illus. article on "Practical Type Making."

Marder, Luse & Co. (951) Chicago Type Foundry. Price List and Printer's
     Purchasing Guide, showing Specimens of Printing Type manufactured
     by Marder, Luse & Co. Foundry; Chicago, 1893 ....$3.50
          Boards, sound, scuffed, 6½ x 4 in., pp.641; contents complete and
in good condition. This foundry in 1893 was owned by the A.T.F. Co., each
branch of which at the time was doing business under the name of its
previous owner. This is the last book to carry the name of M.L.&Co.

National Paper & Type Co. (955) Muestrario de Tipos de Maquineria y
     Materiales de Imprenta. New York: N.P. & Type Co., 31-35
     Burling Slip, January , 1908 .... 4.25
          Cloth, royal 8vo. pp.398; sound; contents complete and in good
condition; entirely devoted to type and material cast in type metals;
all type fonts shown were provided with the necessary Spanish accents.
          The National Paper & Type Co. was formed to represent a group of
manufacturers of paper, types, machinery and printing material, manufacturing in the U. S. and also doing business in Spanish-speaking
America. It is still in existence.

New England Type Foundry (956½) Specimen of Printing Types from the
     N.E.T.F. Henry Willia, No.66 Congress Street, Boston, 1834.........25.00
          Rebound, half morocco, med.8vo; excellent condition, complete.
          This foundry was established in 1824 at 66 Congress Street, moving
to 243 Washington St. in 1855, remaining there until its dispersal
in 1886. Specimen books were issued 1838 and 1841 (G.A. and J.Curtis)
1844 (G.A.Curtis), 1851 and 1855 (Hobart & Robbins), 1855 (N.E.T.F.Co.),
1868 (Chandler, Cousens & Co.) 1882 (A.B.Packard), All these specimen
books seem to indicate that the various owners had quaint tastes in
types and cuts.

New England Type Foundry. Supplement to the Specimen Book of Modern
     Printing Types, Ornaments and Combination Borders, from the
     New England Type and Stereotype Foundry. George A. Curtis,
     Boston, n.d. (circa 1844) 3.25
          Boards, cloth back, 8½ x 10 x 5/16; supplement to the 1841
book; quaint.

Pacific State Type Foundry (958) Type Specimens. Illustrated Price
     List and Displayed Designs. A reference Book and Catalogue of
     Supplies for Printers...carried in stock and sold by the
     P.S.T.F. A. E. Shattuck. W.F.Shattuck. Formerly Hawks &
     Shattuck. Done at 508 Clay Street, corner Sansome. San
     Francisco, n.d. (circa 1899) 3.50
          Cloth, 10 x 6½, pp.xlviii, 200; stout; contents complete and
in good condition; rare.
          This foundry was begun by Hawks & Shattuck at 409 Washington
St. Hawks was instrumental in persuading Marder, Luse & Co. to be
the first to adopt the point system of Fournier, who in 1734 in
France invented the system. A.&S. issued a specimen book in 1889.
The type bodies of the type faces shown in it were cast on the
point system. Curiously, in this H.&S. book of 1889 the bodies of
the type faces shown in it are said to be cast on the "Aliquot System".
When Hawks withdrew from the firm the Shattucks adopted the name
P.S. T.F. The book offered here was the first under the new name.
The foundry, destroyed in the great fire, did not resume.

Palmer & Rey Type Foundry (952). Fifth revised Specimen Book and Price
    List of Printing Material. Established in 1881; incorporated in
    1889. San Francisco, 405, 407 Sansome St., 1892 ....$4.50
    Flexible cloth, $10\frac{1}{4}$ x 7, pp.450, 64; sound, complete
    This foundry was established in 1881 as a branch of the eminent
foundry of Miller & Richard, (Edinburgh, Scotland) and Toronto. This
book was the latest issued. The foundry was sold to the A.T.F.Co. in
1892. This book was used in 1892 in preparing the inventory. Only
the type faces identified by the stamp "Fitted" were made by P.&R.
Those not stamped were made by Eastern type foundries. P.&R. made
an extensive line of printing machinery and material, which are
described and illustrated at end of this book.

St. Louis Type Foundry (962) Price List of Printing Material. Latest
    Type Specimens. St.Louis Type Foundry. St. Louis: Thirs and Vine
    Streets, July, 1887 .... 3.00
    Flexible cloth, $8\frac{1}{4}$ x $5\frac{1}{2}$, pp.24, 205; sound; complete.
    This was the first type foundry established West of the Mississippi.

St. Louis Type Foundry (961) Specimens of Printing Types, Rules,
    Borders, etc., from St. Louis Type Foundry; together with Price
    List of Printing Material. St.Louis, 1893 ....2.50
    Flexible cloth, $8\frac{1}{4}$ x $5\frac{3}{4}$ in. pp.300; sound; complete.

Union Type Foundry (963) Specimen Book and Price List of Copper
    Amalgam Types and Printer's Materials, manufactured by the
    U.T.F., 337 and 339 Dearborn Street, Chicago, n.d. 1889............2.00
    Cloth, $12\frac{1}{4}$ x 9 in., pp.118; sound; complete; pp.1-35 devoted
mainly to machinery and supplies, of an interesting character, now
obsolete; pp.36-80 types of the U.T.F. manufacture; pp.97-118, types
of other foundries.
    This foundry began in 1872. Some of its patented products were
decidedly novel, such as the Baker Brass Rule Ornaments (pp.72-73),
Scenic Combinations (pp.70-71), Arabian (p.65), and others, which are
only to be found in books issued by these originators.

Wells & Webb (629.87) Specimens of Wood Type manufactured by W.&W.
    and for sale at their printers' warehouse No. 18 Dutch Street,
    corner of Fulton, New York, 1854......................................7.50
    Cloth, covers loose, $12\frac{1}{4}$ x $10\frac{1}{4}$ x 1 in; complete; well worth
repairing; has price list and font schemes.
    Darius Wells was the first to cut wood type faces by machinery,
issuing the first specimens of his work in 1828. To accomplish his
purpose, he invented the routing machine, thus superceding the use of
chisels and gouges. Part of his business was the preparing and sale
of engraver's boxwood. Engravers found the Wells routing machine
very time-saving in what is now termed "routing", a term Wells had
invented. For a long time Wells had a monopoly of the wood type
business in the U.S. through the mastery of the routing machine.

Western Type Foundry (967) Specimen Book and Catalogue. Type, Printing
    Machinery and Materials. St. Louis, April 1912 ....3.00
    Cloth, $10\frac{1}{4}$ x 7 in. pp.196; sound; complete and in good condition.
    This is the fifth specimen book of this foundry, which began in
1901.

Western Type Foundry (968) Specimen Book of Type and Rule, manufactured
  by the W.T.F., St. Louis, June 1917 ....$2.50
   Light boards, 10 x 7 in. pp.186, covers loose but not detached;
contents complete and in good condition.
   This foundry was bought by Barnhart Bros. & Spindler in 1918.

White's Type Foundry (969.01) A specimen of Printing Types from the
  foundry of E. White, No. 11 Thames Street, New York, 1821 ....37.00
   Half morocco, newly rebound; complete and in excellent
condition.
   Elihu White began typemaking at Hartford in 1804. He moved to
New York in 1810, issuing a specimen book in 1812. He prospered, open-
ing branch foundries in Boston, Cincinnati and Chicago, all of which
he sold to firms which became successful, and in 1892 were merged
with the A.T. Co. The last owners of the New York type foundry were
Farmer, Little & Co.(See note under Farmer). Specimen books issued
by the Whites are: 1812, 1817, 1818, 1821, 1826, 1829, 1833 (White,
Hagar & Co., 45 Gold St.) 1835, 1839 (John T. White), 1843 (2), 1845,
1849, 1851, 1854 (White & Co.) 1855, 1858 (Charles T. White & Co.),
1860, 1862 (was issued by Farmer, Little & Co.)(See under Farmer)

White's Type Foundry (970.01) Specimen of Modern Printing Types, cast
  at the Foundry of White, Hagar & Co., 45 Gold Street, New
  York, 1835 ....40.00
   Cloth, 10 x 6 x 1¼ ins; sound and in excellent condition.

White's Type Foundry (972) Specimens of Printing Types and Ornaments,
  cast by John T. White, No.53 Cliff Street, New York, 1849..........18.00
   Cloth, 11½ x 9½ x ¾ ins. ; covers loose and scuffed; contents
complete and in good condition except that title signature (4pp.) is
loose; worth rebinding.

White's Type Foundry (629.88) New York Type Foundry Established in
  1810. Specimen Book of Printing Types, made by Chas. T. White
  & Co., 63 and 65 Beekman Street, New York, 1858....................37.50
   Cloth, leather back, 12 x 9½ x 1 in; stout, scuffed; contents
complete and in good condition; advertisements of printing presses
now obsolete at end.

AMERICAN TYPE SPECIMEN BOOKS ISSUED BY PRINTERS

Conner Type Foundry (593.23). Typographic Messenger. Issued by James
  Conner's Sons, Nos.28-32 Centre Street, New York. 2 volumes
  First vol., 1865-1869; second vol. 1870-1873; illus..............$75.00
   Cloth, each, 13¼ x 10 x 1½ in., complete and in good condition,
slightly scuffed. An exceptionally well edited house organ, issued
regularly, quarterly. Because the publishers accepted the advertisements
of equipments for printing plants that did not compete with their own
manufactures, the contents of the Typographic Messenger were as varied
as those of a regular periodical catering to the requirements of the
printing industry. The literary contents are mainly historical, written

by the leading authorities, mostly American. The illustrations (wood cuts) are interesting, showing many machines and tools now obsolete. These volumes are indispensable to historians of the technology of the printing art. Extremely rare.

De Vinne, Theodore Low (629.46). Specimens of Script and Italic types in the Printing Office of Francis Hart & Co., 63 and 65 Murray St., corner of College Place, New York, 1880.............................$4.25
   Paper; 9½ x 6 in., pp.251; cover slightly soiled; contents complete and clean; well worth rebinding; very rare.
   This is one of the earliest type specimen books edited and printed by De Vinne, a junior partner of the firm of Francis Hart & Co. Hart died in 1877, and between that year and 1908 (when DeVinne became sole owner) De Vinne was sole manager. Like all De Vinne's type specimen books this item is a classic. The types are admirably displayed, one size only on a page, each page containing commendations of the printing art by famous authors -- an anthology that proves the extensive reading of our greatest printer, and pride in his occupation.

De Vinne Press (629.123) Historic Printing Types. A Lecture read before the Grolier Club of New York, January 25, 1885, with additions and new illustrations. By Theo. L. De Vinne, New York, The Grolier Club, 1886.. 18.50
   Half vellum, 8¼ x 10¼ ins., pp.110; a sound but slightly soiled copy; contents clean; a finely printed and authoritatively instructive and interesting book. Contains the De Vinne printer mark.

De Vinne Press (629.43) The Roman and Italic Types in the Printing House of Theodore L. De Vinne & Co., 12 Lafayette Place, New York, The De Vinne Press, 1891................................... 18.50
   Cloth; 9½ x 6½ in., pp.145; excellent condition; a finely printed classic among type specimen books; interesting, instructive; has the De Vinne printer mark -- the first used in America.

De Vinne Press (MM -5-66) The Practice of Typography. Plain Printing Types, a treatise on the processes of type-making, the point system, the names, sizes, styles, and prices of plain printing types. By Theodore Low De Vinne, A.M. Second edition. New York: The Century Co., 1902... 3.50
   Cloth, 7½ x 5¼ in. pp.403; good condition. A model text book; authoritative, interesting, thorough, and well printed.

De Vinne Press (629.20) Types of the De Vinne Press. Specimens for the use of Compositors, Proofreaders and Publisher. New York: The De Vinne Press, 1907......................................10.50
   Cloth, 9½ x 6½ ins. pp.449; excellent condition. A book of great value to students of typography. Edited by De Vinne; printed under his supervision; has his printer mark; rare.

Gage (Harry Lawrence), (1026) Applied Design for Printers. A Handbook of the Principles of Arrangement, with brief comments on the periods of design which have most strongly influenced printing. By H. L. Gage. Published by the Committee of Education, United Typothetae of America, 1920... 3.25
   Cloth, 7½ x 5¼ in., pp.71, with numerous illustrations; excellent condition. Mr. Gage is one of the greatest authorities on typographic art and craftsmanship. This is a very instructive and attractive book.

Harpel (Oscar H.), (629.139), Harpel's Typograph or Book of Specimens
  containing useful information, suggestions, and a collection of
  examples of Letterpress Job Printing, arranged for the assistance
  of master printers, amateurs, apprentices and others. By O.H.H.,
  typographic designer and printer. Cincinnati: printed and published
  by the author, 1870...$10.00
    Full morocco; gilt edge., 9½ x 6¼ in., pp.252, with pp.13 of the
advertisements of progressive manufacturers; excellent condition; printed
in colors. This book represents the most advanced exhibit of American
commercial printing in 1870, with a few examples of title pages; very
interesting; rare.

Johnson, Henry Lewis (1031.01) Printing Type Specimens: Standard and
  Modern Types, with notations on their characteristics and uses. A
  guide for printers, advertisers and students of printing. By H.L.
  Johnson, Instructor in Business Printing at Boston University.
  Boston, The Graphic Arts Co., 1924................................... 2.50
    Cloth, 11 x 7 ins. pp.159; excellent condition; stimulating
to students.

Rand & Avery (629.42) Geo. C. Rand & Avery, Printers. Specimens.
  Boston: No.3 Cornhill. Illus. Boston: circa 1869................... 4.00
    Cloth, 10 x 6½ x ½ in.; excellent condition. In 1869 Rand &
Avery were the most extensive and leading printers in Boston. This
book illustrates and describes all their departments and the building
they occupied at corner of Cornhill and Washington Streets. Specimens
of all the types in use in their plant are included.

Rockwell & Churchill (629.41) Specimens of Types used in the office of
  R.&C., stereotypers and printers, 122 Washington Street, Boston,
  1871.. 2.25
    Cloth, 8½ x 6¾ in.; excellent condition. This firm had an
extensive variety of type faces and borders. An interesting and historically
valuable detail of their book is that with each specimen the names of the
type foundry making it is given.

Stewart, A.A. (629.124) Typo: a primer of information about the
  mechanical features of printing types, their sizes, fonts and
  schemes, etc., with a brief description of their manufacture.
  Illus. Compiled by A.A.Stewart, Instructor at School of Printing, North End Union. Boston, 1914................................1.25
    Cloth, 8 x 5 in., pp.42; excellent condition; a well written
text book.

Stanhope Press (726.01) The Book of Specimens of the Stanhope
  Press. Boston: F. H. Gibson Company, 1905........................5.00
    Cloth, 9 x 6 ins. pp.452; excellent condition. In addition to
exhibiting in a craftsmanlike manner the well-selected types used by
this printing office, this book is a thoroughly good text book of
bookmaking. It exhibits and explains the values of book papers, leathers,
cloths, and has numerous examples of book pages with and without music.
The book is a fine example of efficient bookmaking. The writer has never
seen a better text book of bookmaking.

MacKellar, Thomas, Editor (593.15) The Typographic Advertiser, 2 vols.
Illus. Philadelphia, 1855-1897. Issued 1855-1861 by L. Johnson
& Co. 606 Sansome Street; 1861-1866, L. Johnson & Co. (Thomas
MacKellar, John F. Smith, Richard Smith, Peter A. Jordan);
1867-1884, MacKellar, Smiths & Jordan; 1885-1892, MacKellar,
Smiths & Jordan Company (Thomas MacKellar, president; Richard
Smith, vice-president; John F. Smith, treasurer; William Brasher
MacKellar, secretary; George Frederick Jordan, assistant
secretary. William B. MacKellar succeeded his father as editor in
1885. Bound in with above three issues of the T.A. in a smaller
format, dated July 1896, February 1897, issued by the American
Type Founders Co., the latter celebrating the centennial (1796-1896),
containing the history of the foundry, illustrated with portraits
of all the proprietors from 1796 to 1892 and pictures of the
building occupied and owned by L. Johnson & Co., and the last
expanded building, as it was in 1896, under the management of the
A.T.F. Co..(2 vols.)....$225.00
Half morocco, 13 x 10½ in., pp.444 (vol. 1, 1855-1870),
pp.445-984 (vol.2, 1870-1892); perfect condition, newly bound; complete;
extremely rare.

For a thorough appreciation of the achievements of American
typemaking these volumes are indispensable. It is the first house organ
of a type foundry ever published. Its editor from the first to the last
issue, covering a period of thirty-eight years, was Thomas MacKellar,
who became the most famous of American typemakers, and by the abilities
displayed in this house organ -- a combination of thorough technical
knowledge, with literary and poetical genius, and the intuitiveness of
the historian -- made his type foundry the most famous and most extensive
in the world. MacKellar was famous in his day as a writer of verse, of
which some have been published in book formats, and many appear in this
house organ. The history of typography and of many eminent typographers
cannot be fully written without the aid of these volumes. This is a
house organ long disused, yet made so interesting that a typographer
enamoured of his art cannot fail to find it readable on every page -- a
classic among house organs, the interest in which is as great, even
greater, now than when first printed. There is wit and humor in its
specimen lines which evoke smiles as they are read -- an unusual permanent
quality in such compositions, quite different from the usual inanities.
Doubtless, during their actual currency they made many friends throughout
the world and helped to make MacKellar's type foundry famous, besides
attracting customers. Typographically, for many years, especially when
MacKellar assumed full control of the type foundry, the Typographic
Advertiser was flawless in every detail. It is liberally illustrated with
fine wood cuts. This item will charm the most fastidious collector.

MacKellar (Thomas), (593.17) Typographic Advertiser, issued by L. Johnson
& Co. 9 Sansom Street, Philadelphia, 2 vols. Vol.1: 1855-1862,
pp.1-200; vol.ii: 1862-1869, pp.201-412..............................$12.00
Half morocco and cloth; sound, scuffed; contents complete
slightly soiled, but several specimen lines mutilated judiciously by
cut-outs, not impairing the books as records of type faces and prices,
hence the very low price. A student's item.

McMurtrie (Douglas C.), (1169.01) American Type Design of the Twentieth
Century, with specimens of the outstanding types produced during
this period, With an introduction by Frederic M. Goudy, Chicago,
1924.. 1.25
Boards, 9 x 6 in., pp.64; excellent condition.

University Press, Cambridge, Mass. (629.44) Specimen Book of the
     University Press, John Wilson & Son, containing sample pages
     from certain characteristic books manufactured by them. Also
     samples of the various stock, book, and job type faces, foreign
     and music types, head and tail pieces, initial letters, etc.
     Cambridge, Mass., 1900...$6.50
          Cloth, 10 x 12 in., pp.228; excellent condition; has full page
view of this distinguished printing office, facsimile of two of the
earliest imprints of the Harvard University Press (1640 and 1641),
picture of the first printing press used by the latter press (now in
the capitol of Montpelier, Vermont), and an historical sketch; a handsome,
model specimen book.

Page (958.01). Specimens of Chromatic Wood Type, Borders, etc. Wm. H.
     Pa ge & Co. Greenville, Conn. n.d. circa 1875.....................7.00
          Cloth, 18 x 14 x $\frac{3}{4}$ in.; sound, complete, good condition. This is
the most notable of wood type specimens. Page outshone all competitors
in imparting a degree of artistry in designing wood type and borders,
most of which could be printed in several colors. Finely printed in
many colors; a work of unusual excellence, well worth preserving.

(AUSTRIA) Trattner (Joannem Thomam) (1016) Specimen characterum latinorum
existentium in Caesarea ac Regio-Aulica Typorum Fusura, apud J.T.T.,
Caesareo-Regio Aulicum Typographum et Bibliopolam. Vindobonae, mensa
Julii anno 1759 . . . .$4.00
Boards, 9 x 7 x ½ in.; covers loose but not detached; wide margins;
issued by the Imperial Printing Office in Vienna; notice at end is dated
1760.

Hof-und Staats Druckerei in Wien (1016a) Prints uniform in size, on
heavy hand-made paper (22 x 15½ in.), printed in honor of the
visit of the Grand Dukes Nikolaus and Michael of Russia in
1853. The lot, as under, 22 prints, for $2.75
In 1853 and until the fall of the Austrian empire in 1918 the
Imperial Printing House in Vienna was the most advanced in the world.
It was noted for its research work in the impressional graphic arts,
especially in engraving processes. What its status is now this writer
does not know. The prints offered here at nominal cost are (a), The
nations offering homage to Gutenberg; (b), The Imperial Coat of Arms
with a border memorializing printing, art, science, and commerce, the
design beautifully engraved on glass (glassdruck); (c) Entrance to
St. Stephen's Cathedral in Vienna -- wood engraving; (d), Portrait
of the last emperor of Austria, then a youth who reigned as the Great
War began, engraved by the "guillochirung" method (intaglio); (e)
8 ground plans of the printing house -- wood engravings and types;
(f), 16 examples of nature printing, a process that preceded process
engraving in line. This method of plate-making was invented in the
Austrian Imperial Printing Office, where it was much used for re-
producing herbs, other plants and leaves, and especially prepared
cross sections of minerals (quartz, etc.). The results were satis-
factory, but the method is now obsolete, superseded by less trouble-
some methods.

Poppelbaum (1007) Octav-Probe der K.u.K. Hof-Schriftgiesserei Poppelbaum.
Ausgabe 1896, Wien $5.00
Cloth, 10½ x 7½ in., pp.522; good condition, complete; well
printed, with red line page borders.

(AUSTRALIA) Specimen of Type and Borders, cast by F.T. Wimble & Co.,
At their Australian Type Foundry, 87 Clarence St. Sydney,
Feb. 1, 1904 . . . . $1.00
Pamphlet, 8 vo., pp.33. This is the first type specimen book
of the first type foundry established in Australia. Everything
shown in it is copied exactly from foundries of the northern
hemisphere, principally U.S.A.

Wimble (HH-5-67) Specimens. Australian Type and Borders cast
on American Point Lining System. F.T. Wimble & Co., Ltd.,
35-43 Clarence St., Sydney. Warehouses in Melbourne, Adelaide,
Brisbane, Perth. January, 1926 . . . . $4.00
Cloth, 4to., pp.193; complete and in good condition.

(BELGIUM) Plantin (1006) Index Characterum Architypographiae Plantinianae. Specimen des Caracters employes dans l'Imprimerie Plantinienne, avec une Preface par Max Rooses, conservateur du Musee Plantin-Moretus. Antwerp, 1905 . . . . $7.00
    Printed in French and Dutch; specimens printed from the actual types preserved by the descendents of Plantin, as instructed in the will of that great printer, to whom we owe the preservation of the Musee-Plantin-Moretus, one of the most interesting museums in Europe--a veritable printing house and foundry of the olden times. This item is bound in paper, 14½ x 11, 3/8 in., contents complete and in good condition. No.119 of an edition of 200.

(CANADA) Montreal Type Foundry (954) Specimens of Printing Types and Ornaments cast at the M.T.F., corner St. Helen and Lemoin Streets; Montreal, C.T. Palgrave, proprietor. (Agent for Canada West, Mr. D. K. Feeham, Toronto) 1850 . . . . $12.00
    Stamped cloth, 10½ x 7½ x ¾ in., sound; contents clean and in good condition; interesting preface; very rare. Palgrave also issued specimen books in 1 845 and 1865.

(ENGLAND AND SCOTLAND) Caslon (84-1-9) THE SECOND PRINTING OF WILLIAM CASLON'S FIRST SPECIMEN BOOK ISSUED IN THE SAME YEAR AS THE FIRST (1764), WHICH ARE IDENTICAL IN CONTENTS, EXCEPT THAT THIS COPY HAS ANOTHER IMPRINT AND A SLIGHT CHANGE IN THE WORDING OF THE TITLE PAGE. BOTH ISSUES OF 1764 ARE APPARENTLY PRINTED FROM THE SAME TYPES. A Specimen of Printing Types, by Wm. Caslon & Son, Letter Founders, London. Printed by John Towers, 1764. . . . .$110.00
    Leather, 8¼ x 5½ x ½ in.; sound; contents complete and in good condition. NOT IN REED; our copies are apparently unique. The first printing of this specimen was printed by Dryden Leach, a copy of which is in our Library. Reed records a Caslon specimen book, carrying the Leach imprint, dated 1763, a year earlier than our copy. Examination of this Leach 1763 copy proves the 1763 copy to be minus certain signatures, and leads the writer to surmise that W. Caslon & Son, bound up an un-completed copy of the Leach 1764 book, and altered the date to 1763, as a favor to Isaiah Thomas, to whom the book was sent in the latter part of the year 1763, at which time Thomas was the most extensive buyer of types in America. Thomas' practice was to keep the types of the books he published standing, if he expected the works to run into additional editions.
    The acknowledged classics of designing in England are the type faces made by Caslon between 1720 and 1734, exhibited in 1764 for the first time in book form. Their popularity and manufacture continued until early in the nineteenth century, when their manufacture dis-continued and they ceased to be shown in Caslon type specimen books. However, they came into fashion again about 1850, since which date they have become the most popular -- best sellers -- until the present time in all English speaking countries. All specimens issued by the Caslons have become collectors items, and are much sought for by connoisseurs of printing types, a majority of whom regard the ancient Caslon type designs as still unsurpassed -- no type specimen books are rarer.
    Reed, in his History of Old English Letter Foundries lists twenty issues of Caslon type specimens, from 1734 to 1830, all except three of which are in the Typographic Library of the American Type Founders Co. in Jersey City. Of issues prior to 1830 this library owns issues of Caslon's type specimens, NOT IN REED, of following dates:

1734, a broadside, large post, the only known copy of the earliest known specimen issued by Caslon. This was issued from Caslon's Ironmonger Row address. In the same year Caslon changed his address to Chiswell St., which has been the address ever since. The broadside issued from Ironmonger Row was in the same year reissued from Chiswell St. in its identical form, except change of address. Our 1734 broadside is believed to be unique. We refused an offer of $1000.00 for it from the firm of Caslon in 1927. Of items not mentioned by Reed, we have: 1764, Caslon's first type specimen book, one of two editions issued in 1764, one printed by Dryden Leach, the other by John Towers (the duplicate of which is here offered), Because of improvements and enlargements, it is agreed that the Towers edition was later than the Leach. Circa 1766 (22-page book of flowers and combination ornaments -- the most decorative of all the earlier Caslon specimens), printed by T. Wright, Essex St., Strand.

Reed list no books later than 1830, of later dates, we have: 1832, 1833, 1834, 1838, 1840, 1841, 1842, 1843, 1848, 1849(2), 1850(2), 1851, 1854(2), 1857(2), 1862, 1865(2), 1868, 1875, 1890, 1892, 1895, 1908, 1913, 1918, 1920, 1925

Caslon (82-2-14) A Specimen of Printing Types, by William Caslon, founder to his Majesty. No date, but prepared for insertion in Chamber's Cyclopedia, 1784-1786, and dated by Reed (p.256) 1785 . . . . $12.00
Broadside, 8 pp. size of page 17 x 10$\frac{1}{4}$ in; secured in board covers, back fold torn but not detached. Contains specimens of all the products of Caslon at that date (1785) that were cast in type moulds. The specimen of script on p.8 is in the form of a draft and carries the date May 2, 1785. Differs from other Caslon broadsides in that the specimens are arranged in two columns of the page, each column a little wider than 3$\frac{1}{4}$ in; contents in good condition.

Caslon (84-1-24) TWO TITLES (RARE) BOUND TOGETHER, BOTH ITEMS UNKNOWN TO REED. First Title: A Specimen of Printing Types, by Wm. Caslon (111), letter-founder to the King. London: Printed by C, Whittingham, 1796. Second Title: A Specimen of Cast Ornaments, by Wm. Caslon, letter-founder to the King. London: Printed by C. Whittingham, Dean Street, Fetter Lane, 1795. Two titles in one cover $50.00
Half morocco, front page of original board cover bound in, 9$\frac{1}{2}$ x 6$\frac{1}{2}$ x $\frac{1}{2}$ in.; price list, dated Salisbury Square Letter Foundry, January 1, 1796; in good condition and complete.

These specimens were issued by the grandson of the celebrated William Caslon. It contains a dedication to George III. Caslon III seceded in 1792 from the business, established by his grandfather at Chiswell Street, and purchased the foundry established by Joseph Jackson, who had been apprenticed to Caslon I. Wm Caslon III eventually moved to Salisbury Square, a little way from Fleet Street. He was a superior, practical typemaker, and his types were superior to those of his grandfather -- the Caslon Old Style types, now so popular. His specimen books were also superior. In 1803 he took his son William Caslon IV into partnership who in 1819 sold the Salisbury Square Type Foundry to Messrs. Blake, Garnett & Co., the precursors of the firm of Stephenson, Blake & Co., now the leading typefounders in Great Britain.

Caslon (629.90). Caslon & Sons Specimens of Printing Types. (London)
1848 . . . .$ 1.50
Stamped cloth, 9½ x 6½ x 1½ ins., covers loose and detached,
requires and merits rebinding; contents clean and complete, but not
stitched. This is the earliest example we have seen of the worst of
all possible bindings, at the time much used in England, in which to
avoid the expense of stitching, the signatures are glued together on the
back, so that with use they became loose, hence the low price. As
Reed (p.256) does not list any Caslon specimens later than 1830, this
item is not in Reed; it is, nevertheless historically important, as it
marks the beginning of the re-instatement of the now famous Caslon
roman and italics, which had not been shown in the Caslon specimen
books for nearly half a century, during which time they had been
displaced by the modern romans and italics invented by Bodoni in the
last decade of the eighteenth century. None of the romans and italics of
Wm. Caslon, which now are among the best sellers in the typemaking
industry, are shown in this book, but that they were returning to
favor is indicated by an advertisement on the leaf following the
title: "The printers are...informed that in addition to the following
Modern Specimen this foundry includes the works of the justly celebrated
William Caslon I by whom it was originally established...Specimens of
these types of the original Caslon foundry may be seen in Chiswell
Street, but, being nearly out of print, cannot be generally circulated".
Not until Henry W. Caslon (the son mentioned in the title page of this
item) assumed the management, were the discarded type faces included in
the Caslon type specimen books. H.W. Caslon was the last of the Caslon
family; he died in 1874; his successors have adopted the name of Caslon,
Smith being their natal names.

Caslon (983) Specimens of Types and Borders and illustrated Catalogue
of Printers' Joinery and Materials. H. W. Caslon & Co., Ltd.,
82 and 83 Chiswell Street, London E.C., and at Manchester,
England. The preface is dated 1913 . . . .$ 6.00
Cloth, 11½ x 9 x 2¼ ins., complete and in good condition. Has
full page pictures of premises at Chiswell Street and at Hackney,
London.

Caslon (988) Second edition of the item above (dated 1918) . . . .$ 6.00
During the years 1914-1918 the typemaking industry in Great
Britain was about at a standstill, because of the War; hence the
similarity of this item with that of 1913; complete and in good
condition.

Caslon (629.91) Specimens of the Original Caslon Old Face Printing
Types, engraved in the early part of the 18th Century by Caslon I,
n.d. H.W. Caslon & Co., 22 and 23 Chiswell St., London E.C. . . . .$ 2.50
Cloth, 14½ x 10½ in., 11. 16; a complete showing of the celebrated
original Caslon Old Face, issued about 1888 -- the first separate
specimens of these types. This was issued by Thos. W. Smith, who, upon
the death of the last of the Caslon family (H.W. Caslon) in 1874 came
into the ownership of the celebrated type foundry, and conducted under
the firm name as it was in 1874. A well printed document, in good
condition.

Caslon (629.92) H. Caslon & Son. Specimen of Printing Types (stamped
   on cover), n.d. (circa 1840) $1.00
      Cloth, 15½ x 11 in., 11 32 Complete but in poor condition, leaves
loose, desirable to those forming a complete Caslon collection. The
Old Face upon which this foundry built its reputation, is not shown
or referred to. The book begins with an "Address" in which the contents are described as a "Selection of Modern Printing Types". The
Old Face Fonts were in disuse from about 1785 until 1844.

Figgins (993) Specimens of new Book Founts, manufactured by Vincent
   and James Figgins, letter founders, London, 1862 . . . . $3.00
      Stamped cloth, oblong 10 x 12¼ x ¼ in.; good condition and
complete.
      Though only one Figgins duplicate is offered here, this was
an important type foundry, as the collector of type specimen books
should know. The Figgins Type Foundry was established in London in
1792 by Vincent Figgins, who achieved unusual success, and retired
in 1836. His sons, Vincent and James, continued the foundry with
great success, Vincent II retiring in 1885, James in 1868. James II,
who became active in 1856, was head of the firm until his death early
in the twentieth century, soon after which event the business was
discontinued and the plant dispersed. The foundry in 1792 was
situated in Swan Yard, Holborn Bridge; it was moved to West Street,
Smithfield, and thence to Ray Street, Farringdon Road. The building
at the latter address was erected in 1865, and was called the Ray
Street Type Foundry, Under the management of James II the business
became the most extensive in England and maintained an increasingly
high reputation. In 1876 the foundry was greatly enlarged. The firm
was in 1876 the wealthiest and most extensive of the typefoundries
of England. With their wealth the Figgins' appear to have become
careless and unprogressive, so that its trade declined. James II
became high sheriff of the city of London, and member of parliament
for Shrewsbury. A few years after the death of James II an attempt
to recreate the good will was made by the grandson of James I, R. H.
Stevens, who had joined the business in 1881. He did business under
the title of the Southwark Type Foundry, Southwark Street, London,
S.E., from whence he issued a specimen book. The type specimen books
of the Figgins Type Foundryware all animated with a progressive spirit.
They are rare. Issues on our shelves are of dates 1815, 1832, 1835,
1837, 1838(2), 1839, 1841, 1843, 1845(2), circa 1846, 1847(2), 1848,
1849, 1862(2), 1867, 1872, 1873, 1895.

Fry (in frame). A Specimen of Printing Types, made by Joseph Fry and
   Sons, Letter-Founders, Worship Street, Moorfields, London, 1785
   (minus frame) $16.00
      Broadside, 21 x 16½ ins.; in good condition. This type foundry
begun in 1764 in Bristol by Fry and Pine. Joseph Fry was a scholarly
man of means; Pine was a printer and publisher; the foundry was
operated by Isaac Moore; in 1768 the firm name was Isaac Moore at
Bristol. In 1768 the foundry was moved to London where it was conducted
by Isaac Moore and Co.; the "Co" was Joseph Fry, whose name first appears
as proprietor in 1785, the year in which this broadside was issued. This
foundry has an interesting scholarly history. The roman style italics
displayed in this broadside are all old style (modern romans and italics
not then invented), similar but not copies of Caslon's types, to which

they are superior. The name of the firm was changed from time to time; Edmund
Fry & Co., Fry & Steele, Edmund Fry, Edmund Fry & Son; in 1829 it was sold, and
after passing through various ownerships, what remains of it, if it is preserved,
is now in the type foundry of Stephenson, Blake & Co., Sheffield, now the leading type foundry in Great Britain. Edmund Fry, a grandson of the founder, was
the most scholarly type founder of his time in England. Under his management
the foundry achieved great distinction, as reflected in its various specimen
books.   When the fashion for modern style type faces ousted the old style type
faces from the market, he refused to follow the change of fashion, decided to
abandon the type making occupation, and prepared an announcement of that fact
and his reasons for deserting the field. It is a pungent document. He refers
to the modern style of type faces as . "a rude, pernicious, and most unclassical
innovating system", and alluded to the introduction of "fancy letters of anom-
alous forms, with names inappropriate and disgraceful in a profession allied
with scholarship", as injurious and desolating. In scholarship he has left a
monument in his "Pantographia", containing accurate specimens of all the known
alphabets in the world,...forming a comprehensive digest of phonology", pp.356,
published in 1799. It is a great work, on which he employed his leisure time
for sixteen years. None but a devoted scholar, as wealthy as devoted, could
have accomplished such a work; it was sold largely by subscription; two copies
were printed on vellum, one of which is in our library.

Miller & Richard (1003). Selection from the Specimens of Book and Newspaper
        Founts, by M. and R., typefounders to Her Majesty for Scotland,
        Edinburgh and London, 1852...$ 3.50
        Stamped cloth, 12½ x 10 x ½ in.; sound condition; contents complete
and in good condition. Many examples of book pages of the period when printing
was mainly employed in book and newspaper work, and less in commercial work.
This also was the period when Edinburgh excelled all other cities in bookmaking.
        This firm was established by William Miller about the year 1809. Miller
had been foreman for Alex Wilson of Glasgow, the first type founder in Scotland.
Miller died in 1838, since which date the firm name has been Miller & Richard.
Richard became a partner in 1832, though his name did not appear until 1838,
since which year the business has been conducted by members of the Richard
family.
        M. & R. are distinguished by having originated (about 1860), at the
beginning of the revival of the use of old style body type faces, the Modernized
Old Style, roman and italic, with the bold faces thereof called Antique Old
Style, which for book and magazine printing in English-speaking countries still
retain their popularity, and consequently have been reproduced by all the major
type foundries. In the U.S. MacKellar, Smiths & Jordan called their reproduct-
ion (1867) the Bradford Series, and the Dickinson foundry called their repro-
duction (1868) the Franklin Series. The M. & R. Modernized Old Style, roman,
italic, and antique, constitute the chief contribution of Great Britain to the
art of type design, not excepting Caslon Old Style, which is of French origin,
and which had a quite limited use and sale after its revival in 1850, until in
1896 it was discovered to be well adapted and effective for commercial printing.
The M. & R. type foundry, had achieved before 1850 the reputation of using type
metal of the best quality and for many years dominated the demand for magazine
and book types; this superiority was believed to be based on the use of "tea
lead" instead of the pig lead of commerce.   Tea lead is the thin sheet lead
used to protect tea leaves as lining within tea chests; this lead is more highly refined than lead sold in pigs. Early type specimen books of this foundry
are very rare. Of dates other than those listed by Reed (p.356), we have 1835,
1840, 1852 (2), 1857, 1860, 1862, 1866(2), 1868, 1870(2), 1890, 1892, 1895,
1896, 1910.

Wilson (1013.03). A Specimen of Printing Types. Cast in the Letter Foundry
of Dr. Alex. Wilson & Sons. Glasgow, 1783......................$ 12.00
A broadside, 20 x 16½ in., printed on one side only; good condition.
This specimen was issued as a supplement to Chambers-Rees Cyclopedia; the
second Wilson specimen; the first was issued in 1772.

Dr. Alex. Wilson, a graduate and professor of the universities of St.
Andrews and of Glasgow, established the first type foundry in Scotland, in 1742,
in Glasgow. The foundry was well supported and earned a good reputation. In
1760 Dr. Wilson put the control of the foundry in the hands of his two sons,
who did business under the title of the Glasgow Letter Foundry of Dr. Alex.
Wilson & Sons. In 1830 the business was conducted by two grandsons, who in
1832 established a branch house in Edinburgh; in 1834 they transferred the
Glasgow Type Foundry to London in premises in Gough Square; in 1840 a branch
was established in Dublin. In 1845 the surviving grandson, Alexander, failed
and the London foundry became consolidated with the Caslon Type Foundry in 1850.
The foundries in Edinburgh and Dublin were sold to a partnership of Marr, Gallie
& Co., with branches in London and Dublin. In 1874 this business was incorporated as the Marr Typefounding Co., which was active as late as 1892; it has
since been discontinued. In 1812 the Wilsons, in the Glasgow Type Foundry,
issued a specimen book of "Modern-Cut Printing Types". These "Modern-Cut"
types were the first of the modern roman types which proved to be acceptable
to printers and publishers in English-speaking countries; they were and are
now properly described as "Scotch-cut modern roman body types." Scotch-cut
modern roman types were in 1812 accepted as improvements on the modern roman,
designed by Bodoni and Didot. The latter have squared sharp serifs, "Scotch-
cut" serifs are bracketed on the inner sides, this detail removing the sharp
appearance. Prior to 1812 the Wilson types were all old style, resembling those
made by the Caslons. The popularity of "Scotch-cut" modern romans caused the
printers to abandon the use of Old Style romans for more than half a century.
The specimen books of the Wilsons are highly important to students of type
design.

Wilson (1013.01). A specimen of Printing Types, cast in the Letter Foundry
of Alex. Wilson & Sons. Glasgow, 1789............................$ 8.00
Original boards, 9 x 6½ x ½ in., covers detached; contents complete and
in good condition; well worth repairing or rebinding; very rare.

Wilson (629.110). Specimen of Modern Printing Types cast at the Letter
Foundry of Alex. Wilson & Sons. Glasgow, 1833....................$ 7.00
Cloth, leather back, 11½ x 9 x 1½ in., covers detached; contents complete
and in good condition; gilt edges, wide margins; well worth rebinding; interesting preface.

Wilson (629.109). Selection from the Specimen Book of Alex. Wilson & Sons,
Glasgow Letter Foundry, Great New Street, Gough Square, London,1834..$5.00
Stamped calf, 10½ x 8½ x ¾ in., covers loose, but not detached; contents
complete and in good condition; gilt edges; all body types; interesting preface;
well worth repairing. All Wilson type specimen books are impressive.

(FRANCE) Derriey (986). Gravure et Fonderie de C. Derriey. Specimen Album.
Paris, 1862...$22.50
Half morocco, 15 x 12 ins., pp. 187; in good condition, printed on one
side only; contents slightly water stained on margins, specimens not affected;
complete; has price list and two fold broadside issued in 1878 by Jules Derriey,
successor . Of the contents, 44 leaves are printed effectively in several
colors. That Derriey was master of the art of type casting is proved on leaves
112-125, where the perfecting of the fine lines require workmanship excelling
the casting of type faces. The older Derriey was the inventor of the mitering
machine, shown on p.108, with examples of perfect joining of brass and type
metal, impossible of execution without his machine, an apparatus indispensable

in all printing offices. The older Derricy was also the inventor of the typographic numbering apparatus advertised on the inserted broadside. His inventions and his decorative designs were copied immediately in all countries in
which there are type foundries. The price for the above book is very moderate
on account of slight water stains.

A very handsome, finely printed book.

Didot (Firmin), Didot (Jules) and Molo (1092). Specimen des Caracteres de
    MM. Firmin Didot, Jules Didot et Molo -- A broadside 28 x 9½ in.,
    bound in with Manuel de la Typographie Francaise, ou Traite complet de
    l'Imprimerie, ouvrage utile aux jeunes typographs, aux libraires et
    aaux gens de lettres, par P. Cappole, inspecteur de l'imprimerie et de
    la librairies. Paris, 1826...$ 6.00
    Original boards, leather back, 10¼ x 8½ in., pp. (V), 92; sound; contents
complete and in good condition. Frontispiece, portrait of Gutenberg; pp.49-88,
in addition to broadside bound in at end; contains an excellent exposition of
ancient and of the 1826 period, with specimens of designs of Gille, Leger, etc.
--useful for students of typography.

Dupont (Paul), (988). Fonderie de Caracteres. Premier Specimen. Clichey,
    1875.. ....$ 4.00
    Boards, 12 x 9 in., pp. 55; sound; contents complete and clean; pictures
of type foundry and extensive printing establishment on first and last pages
of covers. Paul Dupont was an enthusiastic and successful master printer,
author of a 2-vol. history of printing, an elaborate illus. account of his
typographic establishment in 1867 and the founder of the first profit-sharing
(co-operative) printing office.

Estienne Municipal School of Printing (26). Ecole Municipale Estienne.
    Compsotiion des Langues Orientales par A Laboret. Paris, 1893.....$ 5.00
    Half morocco, 13 x 10 ins., pp. 290, iv, 50; covers and contents in good
condition; 290 pages contain lessons in type compostion for advanced students;
54 pages contain lessons for composition in Arabic, Hebrew Syriac, Assyrian,
Persian Hieroglyphic, Egyptian Hieratic and Demotic, Coptic, Abyssianaian,
Sanscrit, Armenian, Greek, Epigraphic and Chinese alphabets, showing all
characters, with translations in French, and lays of cases to hold all characters. Most valuable to students and the curious in exotic languages, in respect
to which this is a quite valuable book. Apart from the latter considerations
(which induce us to offer the book in this list), this is a desirable text book,
a fine book, the title of which is Essais Progressifs sur la Composition Typographique de Tableau et Travaux de Villes divers. Par V. Breton, professor
technique a l'Ecole Estienne.

    The status of the Ecole Estienne is much more scholarly than is held
by any printing schools in countries other than France. In 1924 the writer
attempted to pay the director of the school a personal visit, having previously inspected every department of it, I was informed that I could not meet the
director on that day, for the reason that he was being installed as a member of
the Academie Francaise, membership in which was the highest honor that could
be conferred upon French men of letters, with a membership of forty ("the forty
immortals").

Poignot (629.105). Fonderie G. Peignot & Fils, 68 Boulevard Edgar-Quinet,
    Paris. Specimen General. Tome 1: Material, Filets, Fantasies Class-
    iques et Modernes, Vignettes, Ornaments. Creations Francaises en
    Typographic Moderne. hors concours; Paris, 1900.................$ 5.00
    Boards, leather back., 10½ x 7½ in., sound; contents complete and in
good condition. For many years the most progressive type foundry in France.
Consolidated since the Great War with the Deberney type foundry (at one time
owned and operated by Balzac), it is now the most extensive foundry in
France. An attractive, well printed book. At end of the book, under the title

of "Retrospective" type faces of various epochs are shown in an interesting
manner, all cast from the original ancient matrices.

(GERMANY) Andreae (978). Proben aus der Schriftgiesserei der Andreaischen
        Buchhandlung in Frankfurt am Main. 1834..........................$30.00
        Original boards, 10 x 6½ x 1 inc., oblong; sound, complete; paper
slightly faded. Preface and announcements in German and French. Price list.

Breitkopf and Ehrhardt (343.01). TWO VERY RARE TYPE SPECIMENS, THE EARLIEST
        KNOWN OF EACH TYPEFOUNDRY, Leipzig, 1739, incorporated in the famous
        and earliest complete text book of typography. First Title: Schrift-
        Probe, oder Kurzes Verzeichniss derjenigen Hebraisch, Greichisch,
        Lateinisch und Teutschen Schriften, welche in Herrn Bernhard Christoph
        Breitkopf's, Schriftgiessery allhier befindlich sind (158 specimens
        on 15 pp.), Leipzig, 1739. Second Title: Gegenwartige Hollandische
        Schriften, und noch andere mehr, in Ehrhardtischen Giessery allheir
        zu bekommen, (29 specimens on 8 pp.) These rare specimens are shown
        on pp. 145-160 and the 8 pp. following of Gessner's (Ch. Fr.),
        Die so nothig als nutzliche Buchdruckerkunst und Schriftgiesserei,
        mit ihren Schriften, etc. Mit einer vorede Herrn Johan Erhard Kappen:
        Leipzig, 1740-1745. 4 vols in two..........................$25.00
        Boards, each vol. 7 x 4½ x 2⅛ ins., vol. 1 sound, vol.II broken on
back; contents complete, profusely and carefully illustrated; poorly.printed as
usual with printing in Germany of this period. Preceding vol. IV is the notable
2-pp. copperplate allegorical of peace and war — Peace represented by a carefully detailed view of a printing office, and War by armed soldiers and artilery.
The interesting, valuable features of these four volumes are too numerous to
describe in this place. We heartily subscribe to the opinion of William Blades,
the leading authority in England on the literature of typography. Blades
writes: "There is no work in any language of greater interest than this to the
student who loves the early history of typography and biographies of celebrated
printers. It is full of portraits, illustrations and out-of-the-way information",
A copy of this work, advertised as being in pristine condition in covers and
contents has recently been offered for $100, which is the value at which we in-
ventory our almost perfect library copy. The defects in binding of the duplicate copy offered here may easily be remedied by a careful binder, though they
induce a very low price. Contents are complete.

Brockhaus (629.95). Title on cover: Proben von F. A. Brockhaus, Schriftgiesserei
        Schriftschneiderei und Stereotypie, in Leipzig. Begins with broadside:
        Preiscourant de Schriftgiesserei von F. A. Brockhaus in Leipzig.
        Mai, 1854...$20.00
        Original boards, cloth back, 12 x 9¼ in., pp. 251, sound, contents
complete and in good condition, interesting, characteristic of the period,
especially the cuts.
        The firm of F. A. Brockhaus in Leipzig was established in 1805. It
now confines itself to printing and publishing, and no longer conducts a type
foundry. It celebrated its centennial in October, 1905, and ranks high in the
publishing profession. Brockhaus type specimen books on our shelves are dated
1846, 1854, 1859.

Dennig, Finck & Co., (985).   Dennig, Finck & Co. Schrift und Stereotypen-
        Giesserei in Pforzheim. Probe-Abdrucke. Erste Abtheilung: Fraktur,
        Feete Fraktur, Gothisch. 1840..............................$1.50
        Boards, 9½ x 6½ x ¼ in.; sound, complete and in good condition.

Dresler (Fr.) und Rost-Fingerlin. Auszug aus den Schrift-Proben der Schrift-
        schneiderei, schrift-stereotypen, und metal-buchstaben-Giesserei, von
        Fr. Dresler und Rost Fingerlin in Frankfurt-a-M. August, 1840...$2.50
        Boards, cloth back, 8½ x 6½ x ½ in.; sound, contents slightly stained.

This foundry was later on owned successively by Dresler, Meyer and Flinsch.
Its specimen books on our shelves are dated: 1837, 1840, 1850, 1852, 1858
(Meyer), 1859, (Flinsch), 1869, 1870, 1871, 1872, 1886, 1889, 1896, 1898, 1899,
1900, 1901, 1903, 1904, 1923, -- and interesting progressive succession of
which we offer several duplicates under the name of Flinsch.

Erhardt,Leipzig, 1739. See Brotkopf and Erhardt, above; also Zinckens and
Erhardt, below.

Flinsch (995). Schrift-Proben der Schriftgiesserei, Flinsch, Frankfort A.M. and
St. Petersburg, 1899..$ 4.00
Original stamped boards, cloth back, 11 x 7½ in. pp. 445, XXXX; good
condition, contents complete. Interesting and exceedingly well printed. Has at
end illustrated catalogue of German printing house machinery and materials.

Genzsch & Heyse. Schriftproben der Schriftgiesserei in Hamburg. No date
(Circa 1893)...$ 4.00
Boards, cloth back, 9½ x 7 x 1½ in., good condition inside and out;
contents attractive and original and well printed.
Established in Hamburg in 1833, this is one of the best esteemed progressive firms in Germany. The present head of the firm is Herr Hermann J.
Genzsch, who was chiefly instrumental in introducing in Germany the French
point system of type borders and the lining system suggested by Herr Hermann
Smalian, a proofreader in Berlin, and first used in the manufacture of types
in St. Louis, by the Inland Type Foundry. The two editions of the specimen
books offered here were ably edited by H. J. Genzsch, who had the advantage
of gaining experience upon completing his apprenticeship, by working in type
foundries in France and the United States in his wanderjahre.

Genzsch & Heyse (629.101). Proben von Schriften, Initialen und Verzierungen.
Schriftgiesserei Genzsch & Heyse. Hamburg, 1902...............$ 4.00
Cloth, 8 x 5½ in., pp. 536; sound and in good condition. Has 2-page
view of the foundry in Hamburg. Has an exceedingly instructive 7-pp. introduction, clearly explaining the French (Didot) point system and the Smalian-
American lining system and other details of typemaking, of which printers
should be advised -- in those respects this book excels all other European
type specimen books.

Klinkhardt (629.103). Gesamt-Probe der Schriftgiesserei Julius Klinkhardt in
Leipzig und Wien. Stereotypie Utensilien. Xylographie. Galvanoplastik. Oktav-ausgabe, 1883..............................$ 6.00
Stamped cloth, 10½ x 7½ ins., pp. Xl, 496; complete, in good condition; beautifully printed, interesting. The Klinkhardt foundry was
successor to a foundry established by B Scholter, during the first half of the
nineteenth century; this he completed modernized, as his specimen books prove.
This book particularly shows leadership in decorative materials.

Klinkhardt (629.102). Schriftgiesserei Julius Klinkhardt, Leipzig, Wien.
Messinglinienfabrik (brass rules), Stereotypie, Galvanoplastik.
1890..$ 4.50
Stamped cloth, 10½ x 7½ ins., pp Lii; complete, in good condition,
except that the first signature is loose; a handsome, well printed book; not
a repetition of the 1883 specimen -- practically a supplement to it; many cuts,
characteristically German and well engraved.

Scholter & Giesecke (630.101). Muster-Sammlung von J. G. Scholter & Giesecke,
Schriftgiesserei, Messinglinienfabrik, Galvanoplastic..Machinenfabrik.
1886..$5.00
Stamped cloth, 10½ x 7¼ ins., pp. 359, (42 pages assigned to printing
office equipment); sound, slightly scuffed; contents complete and in

good condition. This is one of the greater type foundries and printers' supply houses in Germany. It was established in 1819; it is now owned and operated by members of the Giesecke family.

Schramm. Illustrations used by the Printers of the Incunabula. (Der Bilder-
    schmuck der Fruhdrucke). Compiled by Prof. Dr. Schramm, Director of the
    German Book Museum in Leipzig, as follow:
No. 1 (383). Die Drucke von Albrecht Pfister in Bamberg, pp. 7, 305 reproduct-
    ions on 38 plates; half leather. Leipzig, 1922. (publisher price,
    30 marks),,,,,..$ 6.00
No. 4 (382.01). Die Drucke von Anton Sorg in Augsburg, pp. 72, 3096 reproduct-
    ions on 382 plates; half leather. Leipzig, 1922. (Publisher's price,
    210 marks)..$42.50
No. 5 (283). Die Drucke von Johann Zainer in Ulm, pp. 20, 501 reproductions on
    92 plates; half leather. Leipzig, 1923. (Publisher's price, 60 marks).
                                                        ....$12.50
No. 6 (383.02). Die Drucke von Konrad Dinckmut in Ulm, pp. 19, 682 reproduct-
    ions on 107 plates; paper. Leipzig, 1923. (Publishers price, 60 marks)
                                                        ....$12.50
No. 7 (483.03). Die Drucke von Lienhart Holle, Johannes Reger, Johann Schaeffler,
    und Hans Hauser in Ulm, pp. 15, 407 reproductions on 116 plates; paper.
    Leipzig, 1923. (Publisher's price, 65 marks).....................$13.00
No. 8 (384). Die Kolner (Cologne) Drucker, pp. 28, 956 reproductions on 198
    plates; half leather. Leipzig, 1924. (Publishers price, 150 marks).
                                                        ....$ 28.00
No. 9 (385). Die Drucker in Esslingen, Urach, Stuttgart, Reutlingen, Tubingen,
    Blaubeuron, pp. 22, 804 reproductions on 129 plates; half leather.
    Leipzig, 1926. (Publisher's price, 88 marks)....................$18.00
No. 10 (386). Die Drucker in Lubeck: Die Beiden Bruder Brandis, pp. 8, 493
    reproductions on 94 plates; half leather. Leipzig, 1927..........$10.00
No. 11 (389). Die Drucker in Lubeck; Steffen Arndes, pp. 12, 1084 reproductions
    on 181 plates; half leather. Leipzig, 1928.....................$20.00
No. 12 (387). Die Drucker in Lubeck: Ghotan, Mohnkofdrucke, die Drucker in
    Magdeburg, pp. 13, 710 reproductions on 109 plates; half leather.
    Leipzig, 1929..$12.50
No. 13 (388). Die Drucker in Leipzig und Erfurt, pp. 7, 339 reproductions on
    67 plates; half leather. Leipzig, 1930........................$9.50
No. 15 (390.1). Die Drucker in Mainz; Erhard Reuwich, Jakob Meydenbach, und
    Peter Friedberg, pp. 7, 1142 reproductions on 134 plates; half leather.
    Leipzig, 1932...$15.00
    Each item in the above series (Nos.1-13 and 15) is complete and in
good condition. This series affords the only existing practicable means of
completely appraising the literary and artistic ability of the various crafts-
men employed by the various printers active in Germany in the incunabula period.
This collection is of great value to all who are interested in incunabula printings.

Tauchnitz (240). Karl Taugott Tauchnitz, buchhandler, buchdrucker und schrift-
    giesser zu Leipzig; together with a facsimile reproduction (leaves 1-24)
    of his first type specimen book (Proben aus der Schriftgiesserei von
    Karl Tauchnitz in Leipzig, 1825). By Heinrich Schwartz. Berlin 1924.
                                                        ....$5.00
    Original boards, 14 x 10 x 3/8 in., in good condition, with portrait
of Tauchnitz and price list of 1825. Pages 24-26 of the specimen book of
1825 are omitted, containing specimens of borders only.

Woellmer (629.11). Muster & Sammlung von Wilhelm Woellmer's Schriftgiesserei
    und Messinglinienfabrik, Stempleschneiderei Gravir-Anstalt. Berlin,
    S. W., 1894 ....$ 6.00
    Cloth, 11½ x 8½ ins., pp. XVl, 24, 407; good condition, complete. This
        foundry was established in 1840; contents are interesting, especially
the decorative materials and lively cuts; has at end, pp. 369-407, a great and
excellent variety of type faces in the Russian, Greek, Cyrillic and Siamese
alphabets; may be recommended to letterers and commercial art students.

Zinckens and Ehrhardt (304.02). TWO VERY RARE TYPE SPECIMENS INCORPORATED IN
    GESSNER (Chr. Fr.), DER IM BUCHDRUCKEREI WOHL UNTERRICHTETE LEHR JUNGE;
    Leipzig, 1743. First Title: Abdruck: oder verzeichniss derjenigen
    Teutschen Schriften, welche in der Ehrhardtischen Schriftgiesserei
    allhier befindlich sind. Leipzig, 1743; pp. Xll, 44 specimens. Second
    Title: Abdruck einiger Schriftt-Proben und deren Rahmen, wie solche zu
    Wittenberg in C. Zincken's Giesserey...befindlich sind;; pp. XVl, 72
    specimens. The specimens are bound in with the rare text book by Gessner,
    the title of which is given above. The complete collection.....$12.00
        Stout boards, 7 x 4¼ x 1½ ins., sound; contents complete and in good
condition; poorly printed, as usual with books printed in Germany in that period.
This is the first text book in any country planned for apprentices. As a text
book it is in the same class as Moxon's of 1683 of which it is true that the whole
art of typography, if it were forgotten, might be reinstated if a copy survived,
because of its completeness and explicitness. Gessner's text book is more detailed. It is illustrated with two copperplate engravings (a frontispiece allegorical of typography, with an interior view of a printing office in background,
a 3-fold broadside of the lays of type cases for the German, Polish, Latin, Greek,
Arabic, Hebrew, Syrian, alphabets and Calendar signs) and numerous wood engravings. To the text book of 490 pages there is added the play, Deposito Cornuti
Typographici, which was enacted as the main part of the ceremony of advancing the
apprentice to printing to the status of a journeyman: this occupies 62 pp.
addition, which are followed by 50 pp. of appreciation in verse of the art of
printing and its inventors. A book compiled by C. F. Gessner of Leipzig, and
printed by him in 1743.

(HOLLAND). Enschede (989). Epreuve de Caracteres,qui se fondet dans la Nouvelle
    Fonderie de Caracteres de Isaac & Jean Enschede a Haarlem. Deuxieme
    edition augmentee. Augmentee et amelioree jusqu' a l'an 1748...$50.00
        Original marbled paper, 8½ x 5½ x 3/8 in.; sound, but scuffed; contents
complete and in good condition; has portrait of Coster; the second specimen book
of this celebrated foundry; has a historical preface. A copy of this item was
catalogued for sale at eighteen guineas. It is very rare.
        The Enschedes purchased this foundry in 1743 from the heirs of Rudolphe
Wetstein of Amsterdam. It has been owned and operated by the Enschede family
in Haarlem ever since. The Enschedes were printers in Haarlem in 1703 and continued there as printers and type founders until the present time. Enschede
type specimen books are very rare and the contents of them unusually interesting,
as they from time to time acquired the type faces of the earlier foundries. Our
Library has Enschede specimen books, in addition to those listed here, as follows:
1757, 1768, 1806, 1824, 1830, 1836, 1841, 1850, 1855, 1867, 1870, 1883, 1889,
1891, 1894, 1895, 1897, 1902 (2), 1907, 1917, 1925, 1926 (2), 1928, 1930, various
pamphlet specimens 1895-1928.

Enschede (990) (THREE TYPE SPECIMEN BOOKS OF GREAT RARITY BOUND TOGETHER, THE
    PRINCIPAL ITEM -- THAT ISSUED IN 1768 -- IS UNEXCELLED AMONG SPECIMEN
    BOOKS OF ANY PERIOD FOR HISTORIC AND TECHNICAL INTEREST AND VARIETY OF
    CONTENTS). There are three titles, two of which are included in item

71 of the sales catalogue of Birrell & Garnett, of 1928 -- (the classic catalogue of typefounders' specimens and works on typefounding and printing, the notes of the various rare items constituting a veritable history of typefounding.) First title: Proef van Letteren, welke googooten wordern in de Neiwe Haarlemsche Lettergietery van J. Enschede. (Copperplate vignette, engraved in 1741 by A. Van der Laam, an allegory celebrating the invention of typography in Haarlem, with carefully and accurately detailed view of a printing office in the background, with tools used in printing and bookbinding in foreground). 1768, followed by copperplate portraits, each full-size, occupying one leaf, of Joannes Enschede, Coster, Hadrian Junius (originator of the Coster Legend), J. M. Fleischman (the most celebrated of letter-punch cutters), and a view of the Coster monument erected in 1740 by Enschede, and still standing in the rear of the Enschede foundry; also a 32 p. history of the foundry and its predecessors and its more notable employees; to which is added a Second Title: OUDE HOLLANDCHE LETTEREN ZYNDE EERSTELINGEN DER BOEK-DRUKKONST, (showing on 3 leaves, with full-page frontispiece, these probably included with the title (1768) des-cribed above, showing the characters (A to Z, a to z) and the ligatures and abbreviaturen characters, as used by scribes before the invention of printing, and by the earlier printers; these fonts cast in lead matrices said to have been made in the period 1470-1480, which had come into the possession of the Enschedes -- the oldest types in existence. It is a well authenticated fact that the matrices used by the earlier printers were driven in lead; Mappa, the first typefounder in N. Y. City (1791), brought his equipment, then two generations old, from Delft, Holland, and we have in our Library proof that it contained some fonts of lead matrices.) Third Title: VERMEERDERING VAN MEEST NIEUW GESNEDENE LETTEREN IN DE HAARLEMSCHE LETTER-GIETERY VAN JOHANNES ENSCHEDE, ZEDERT 1768, tot 1773. (16 pp. show-ing additions to type faces, created since 1768, (issued as a separate pub-lication in 1773. See Bigmore & Wyman, p. 206). Also, following third title, an 8 pp. price list alphabetically arranged, and at the end a folded broadside, $12\frac{1}{2}$ x $8\frac{1}{4}$ in., view of the interior of the Enschede foundry, showing all processes of typemaking, carefully drawn and detailed by Van Noorde in 1768. Perfect as described.............................$135.00
Original marbled boards, leather back, $8\frac{1}{3}$ x $5\frac{1}{4}$ x $\frac{3}{4}$ in., sound with contents complete and in good condition; illustrations on copper, by celebrated artists. As specimen books they are remarkable in having the names and sizes of each font in Dutch, French, English and German, and adding the names of the famous letter-punch cutters attached to each specimen, with the dates of finishing the work. With Fleischman there were associated Van Dyke and Rosart. Some of the type designs were completed before the Enschede foundry was established. The known and conjectural sources of the material owned at present by the Enschedes extend back to the fifteenth, sixteenth, seventeenth, and early eighteenth centuries, as demonstrated by a diagram prepared by present members of the firm. The price list, in Dutch stuivers, is the most complete we have seen in the earlier type specimen books, and explains the prices in foreign currency. Each page is com-posed within a border, the use of which is seldom repeated. The composition is well done and the presswork admirable. In every generation the Enschedes were dominated by thorough scholars, a fact that accounts for the masterly editing of their type specimen books. The estimation in which these books are held is proved by the fact that their specimen books of 1748 and 1757 are priced at eighteen guineas each by Messrs Birrell & Garnett of London in their masterly catalogue of 1928, and the price of the 1768 specimen book, without the issue of 1733, was twenty-five pounds. Comparison of the contents of our 1768 with theirs indicates that our copy is much more complete.

49

Enschede (629.97) Letterproef van Joh. Enschede en Zonen, lettergieterij te
        Haarlem. Deel ii, Fantasie Letter. Mei 1889..............$6.00
        Cloth, 15 x 11½ in., 184 leaves; contains types used for commercial and
social purposes; covers slighlty cracked at back, but not detached; contents in
good condition; interesting; complete.

Tetterode (1009), Proeve van Letteren, van N. Tetterode, lettergeiter te Rotter-
dam. Erste Gedeelte. 1852 (January)...............................$ 5.00
        Cloth, 4to., ¾ in. thick; sound; contents complete and in good condition.
Tetterode moved to Amsterdam shortly after issuing the 1852 specimen. His
successors named the foundry the Lettergieterij Amsterdam voorheen N. Tetterode.
It is now the most progressive and active type foundry in Holland. Of this
foundry we have, in addition to the items listed in our duplicate specimens, of
dates 1856, 1857,-1864 (5 supplements in one vol.), 1860 (catalogue of matrices
and specimen of word characters in Chinese), 1865 (Egyptian hieroglyph characters),
1860-1874 (collection of broadside specimens, price lists, etc.), 1907, 1908, 1909,
1910, 1919, 1920.

Tetterode (1010.01). Catalogue raisonne de Types Egyptiens Hieratiques de la
        Fonderie N. Tetterode a Amsterdam, 1865.....................$ 5.00
        Boards, 4to., pp. viii, 40 and broadside with specimens of 376 characters,
specially designed by W. Pleyte, under supervision of M. Francois Chabas, this is
evidence of the scholarly enterprise of Tetterode.

Tetterode (1011). Proeve onzer Plantijn-Serie (specimen of a type family named
        Plantin). Deze lettersoorten worden gegeten door de Lettergieterij
        Amsterdam voorheen N. Tetterode, 1912.......................$ 2.00
        Boards, 4to., pp. 74, illus; good condition; an admirable exposition in
black and white and colors of a type design of wide adaptability; with price list
and (on p. 64) an exterior view of the type foundry erected in 1912.

Tetterode (1011.01). Hollandsche Mediaeval een Boek-en Fantaisie Letter door
        S. H. DeRoos. Amsterdam en Rotterdam. Lettergieterij Amsterdam voorheen
        N. Tetterode, 1919..$ 1.50
        Pamphlet, 4to., ¼ in. thick; admirable specimen of a classic type family
in black and colors, including initial letters and decorative materials; in good
condition.

(ITALY) Bodoni (407 a). Sonetta (broadside, 16⅓ x 12 in.)., All'Egregio Filandro
        Cretense l'amico, e parente Euricirete Acrisionos. Parma: Co' typi
        Bodiana, Ottobre 1808 (Brooks 1044)........................$3.00
        Bodoni's books in the days of his greater fame were of a typographic
purity in which borders and decorative material were seldom used. Contemporan-
eous with his books he issued an extensive series of broadsides, which together
were the more attractive products of his printing house, generally decorative.
Examples of these are much more rare than his books. Most of these were comp-
limentary to his personal friendships and to patriotism toward members of the
Bonaparte family. All are very rare.

Bodoni (407 b). Sonetta (broadside, 18 x 13 in.). Omaggio A.S.M. Maria Luigia,
        principessa Imperial, archiduchessa d'Austria. By Canonico Platostainer,
        P.A. Parma: Co' tipi Bodoniana, 1831.......................$3.00
        This was printed after the death of Bodoni at a time when his widow con-
ducted the printing house and fully sustained its reputation. Maria Luigia was
the second spouse of Napoleon the Great, whose memory is revered in Parma to
this date, because of her charities.

Congregation de Propagando Fide (1017). Specimen Characterum Typographei S.
    Concillii Christiano nomini Propagando santissimo Domino nostro Gregorio
    XV1 Pont. Max., idem typographeum invesenti oblatum. Romae, 1843.
    Very rare...$50.00
    Original boards, cloth back, 14 x 9½ x 5/8 in.; sound but slightly
scuffed; contents complete and in immaculate condition.
    This is the most complete polyglot type foundry ever assembled. It
began in Rome in 1626, but soon acquired the polyglot matrices of two other
type foundries belonging to printing houses maintained by the papal see, one of
which was established in 1587, under the management of Paulus Manutius, son of
Aldus, under the name of Stampa Vaticana. Beginning in 1629 this foundry issued
a series of specimen pamphlets of exotic types made and used for printing for
missionary purposes, continuing until into the latter half of the nineteenth
century, about fifty in all. These were generally of small 8vo format. The item
here offered is an edition de luxe. It has 22 pp. of type specimens of Linguae
Asiatica, 27 pp. of more unusual Linguae Europeae, 4 of Linguae Africanae, and
3 pages of Linguae Americanae (Mexican, Algonquin and Peruvian). The book is
beautifully printed, wide margins, printed on one side only -- the finest product
of the printing house of the Congr. de Propaganda Fide. Each specimen is within
a border. The more unusual of the types exhibited are: Samaritan (2), Mandaica,
Chaldaica (3), Tairanica, Syriaca (4), Persica (2), Indostanica (2), Curdica,
Iberica, Brahmanica, Malabarica, Tibetana, Birmanica, Grecian, (16- a varied
exhibit), Hibernica (Irish Celtic), Illyrica (3), Russian. Where the Latin type
characters are used in unfamiliar languages, such as Bosnian, Albanian, Hungarian,
etc., the special accents are shown and also any special characters used. Of
great value to the language student. In this, foundry Bodoni acquired his extensive knowledge of languages.

Societa Augusta-Torina (1108). Caratteri per Biglietti Visita, Circolari, e
    Lavori Commerciel. Nebiola & Cie, Societa August, Turin, 1920...$1.25
    Pamphlet, 48 pp., exquisitely printed, in good condition. At the time
this was printed Signor Lobetti-Bodoni, grand nephew of the famous Bodoni was
managing director of this foundry.

Zatta (83-2-41). Saggi dei caratteri, Vignette e Fregi (Type faces, ornaments
    and borders), della nuova fonderia di Antonio Zatta e Figlio, tipo-
    grafi, caleografi, e libraj Veneti: Venezia, 1794. Con approvazione.
    Very rare...$70.00
    Original vellum, 9½ x 7 in., 62 pp. (50 printed on one side only);
sound, contents complete and in immaculate condition. Has a 13 pp. dedication
to printers and lovers of the arts of typography of much historic and technolog-
ical interest. In 1794 this was the leading house in Venice connected with the
typographic arts; it continued for more than a century. Birrell & Garnett
advertise a 1794 specimen of Zatta for sixteen guineas.

MISCELLANEOUS TYPOGRAPHICA

Advertisements of XV century Printers (261). Buchhandleranzeigen des XV jahrhun-
    derts. Herausgegeben von Konrad Burger. Leipzig, 1907........$18.00
    Stout stamped portfolio, 17½ x 13 x 1 in., in sound condition, slightly
cracked on back; contents in good condition, 32 facsimiles mounted on full size
card boards, with notes. Facsimile 3 is an advertisement of Peter Schoeffer,
Mainz, 1469, containing the first specimen line of types ever used for advertising
purposes; most interesting collection; rare.

Block Printing (297.10). Les Xylographies des XiV et du XV Siecle, au Cabinet
des Estampes de la Bibliotheque Nationale, par P.A. Lemoisne, conservateur du Cabinet des Estampes. Paris, 1927. 2 vols.........$24.00
Paper, 15 x 11, pp. 178 (vol.1), 148 (vol. 2), 130 reproductions in
color with notes; a fine production.

Caslon House Organ (A9). Caslon's Circular, vol. 1, Nos. 1, 1875 to 52, 1889.
Published quarterly; complete.............................$4.00
Original half leather, quarto (12½ x 10 in.); complete. A history
from quarter to quarter of this famous type foundry, reporting its progress and
the status of the typographic arts, domestic and foreign, with specimens and
advertisements of all new type faces and printing office equipments. It is in
fine condition, except that the binding is in the futile unstitched detachable
style then commonly used in England -- hence the extremely low price. American
type styles and printing machinery were in these years successfully entering the
British market. The editorial tone is generally anti-American, though in an
early issue it is acknowledged that American commercial printing was superior.
The fact was that in 1875 American had achieved a superiority in type faces and
printing office equipments which it has since decisively retained. A very interesting publication.

Deutschen Buchgewerbevereins (629.125). Antiqua oder Fraktur (Lateinische oder
Deutsche Schrift), eine kritische studie von Dr. August Kirschmann,
professor of philosophy at the University of Toronto, Leipzig,1921.$1.50
Paper, 6½ x 4½ in., pp. 116; good condition. A scholarly discussion
of the controversy, keen in Germany, of the relative merits of the gothic
(German) characters and the roman (Latin) characters. The types called roman in
English speaking countries are names antiqua in Germany.

Early English Printing (629.143). Early English Printing a series Facsimiles of
all the Types used in England during the XV century with some of those
used in the printing of English books abroad, with an introduction by
E. Gordon Duff. London, 1896. Edition limited to 300 copies.
Printed in Fell Types at the Oxford University Press............$5.00

Gutenberg Gesellschaft (1062.01). Die Entstehung der Frakturschrift, by Rudolf
Kautsch. Mainz, 1922...$1.00

Laville (15.05). L'Imprime de Publicite. Tome 1; Les Elements. By Laville,
ingenieur, conseil E.S.E., Paris, 1926..........................$3.00
Paper 13 x 10 in., pp. 447; good condition, uncut. Examples done in
France and Great Britain and the U.S., illustrating technique, classics, vari-
ations, design, similitudes, decoration, illustration -- a wealth of material
for imaginative students of commercial art.

MacKellar, Smiths & Jordan (1086). 1796-1896. One Hundred Years. MacKellar,
Smiths & Jordan Foundry, Philadelphia. 1896...................$3.50
White stamped linen, 15 x 11½ in., pp. 96; good condition, but slightly soiled. A history of this, the oldest type foundry in America,
with protraits of all the partners, views of the premises occupied, and of all
departments in operation in 1896; printed in the printing office of the foundry.
A special font of type was cut for this book -- 15-point Ronaldson Old Style
Roman, the only font on 15-point body ever cast. All the operations of type
making are illustrated. The contents are in mint condition. In 1806 this
foundry became the owners of the typemaking apparatus brought from Paris to
Philadelphia in 1785, as narrated in this history.

Morison (1137), Four Centuries of Fine Printing (Upward of 600 Examples), of
          the work of presses established during the years 1500 to 1914, with
          Introductory text and indexes by Stanley Morison, London, 1924...$47.50
          Half linen 18½ x 13 x 1½ in., complete and in good condition; No. 305
of 390 copies, perfectly printed at the University Press, Cambridge, England.
A treasury of typographic masterpieces by the masters of typography during
four centuries; beautiful and inspirational; now rare. Publishers price,
10 guineas.

Reed.(629.134). A History of the Old English Letter Foundries, with Notes,
          historical and biographical, on the Rise and Progress of English Typo-
          graphy. Illus. By Talbot Baines Reed, London, 1887............$12.00
          Cloth, leather back, 10 x 8 in., pp. XIV, 379; complete and in good
condition. This is the only complete history of typemaking in any country. It
is authoritative and notably complete -- a recognized classic. T.B. Reed was a
type founder, an authority, and the first secretary of the London Bibliographical
Society.

Rodenberg (704). Julius Rodenberg. Deutsche Pressen: eine Bibliographie. Mit
          vielen schriftproben. Amalthea Verlag, Wien, 1925............$18.00
          Cloth, 9½ x 6¾ in., pp. 350, with 50 full page specimen pages of the
works and types of the leading German private presses, and 16 full page advertisements of private presses. As was to be expected from Rodenberg this work is
thorough, affording complete knowledge of the subject. The book is in mint condition.

(SPAIN)(336). Geschichte de Spanischen Fruhdruckes in Stammbaumen. von Konrad
          Haebler. Leipzig, 1923, With 489 reproductions............$70.00
          Cloth, 16¾ x 13 in., pp. 446; complete and in good condition. An admir-
able work, from which a thorough knowledge of printing and printers in Spain may
be learned; also the types and decorative materials used. An item thorough in
all respects.

Silbermann (629.162). Album Typographique, publie a l'occasion de la Quatrieme
          Fete Seculaire de l'Invention de l'Impreimerie, par G. Silbermann,
          imprimeur a Strasbourg. Strasbourg, Juin 24, 1840............$2.00
          Stitched, not bound, 13 x 10 x ½ in., curious, interesting souvenir of
what was a great occasion in Europe; requires binding; contents complete; margins
wide, permit trimming, to make this good item for a fastidious collector.

Wood (36-2-21). J.& R.M.Wood's Typographic Advertiser. vols.1-7, in two volumes.
          Printed and published quarterly by J. & R.M. Wood (typefounders).
          London, 1862 - 1868...$10.00
          Half leather. front cover of vol. 1 cracked but not detached, 12½ x 10 x
          2 in. (vol.1) and ¾ (vol.2); contents complete and in good condition.
The first house organ of a type foundry published in England. This foundry was
established in 1815 by Richard Austin, a distinguished letter punch cutter; in
1824 his son succeeded to the business; on the death of the son he was succeeded
by R.M. Wood, in partnership with S. and T. Sharwood, under the name of the
Austin Type Foundry; upon the death of all the partners in 1856 the foundry was
sold at the auction to close the estate; it came into the possession of the sons
of Wood, and continued until about 1894, the last partnership under the style
of Austin, Wood, Browne & Co., Austin Type Foundry, Islington, London, N.
          These volumes are essential to a knowledge of the status of the typo-
founding and printing industries in England in the sixties; they contain speci-
mes of all the type faces and cuts made by the publishers; very interesting and
informative; rare